Washington Grangers Celebrate a Century

by
Gus
Norwood

By Gus Norwood

Columbia River Power for the People

Washington Grangers Celebrate a Century

Washington Grangers Celebrate a Century

by
Gus
Norwood

Washington State Grange • Seattle, Washington

Published in the United States
by the Washington State Grange
3104 Western Avenue, Seattle, Washington 98121-1073

Printed in the United States of America
First edition

Uncredited photographs are from the historical files of the Washington State Grange and *The Grange News*. Photograph on pages 2-3 is courtesy of the Washington State Apple Commission.

Book design by Dave Howard and Bill Thorness
Typesetting by *The Grange News*
Book layout by Dave Howard

Library of Congress Catalog Card No.: 88-50556

Library of Congress Cataloging-in-Publication Data

Norwood, Gus, 1916-
Washington Grangers Celebrate a Century

Includes index and bibliography
1. Washington State Grange—History. 2. Agriculture—Washington (State)—Societies, etc.—History. I. Title.
HD1485.W373 338.1'06'0797—dc 19 88-50556

CONTENTS

FOREWORD

The reader of Gus Norwood's fine centennial description of the Washington State Grange will discover, or rediscover, the one-hundred-year history of one of our state's most broadbased and progressive citizens' groups. As a member myself, I'm proud to share this heritage and appreciate Washington State Grange Master Ray Hill's gracious invitation to be a part of this important effort.

The 19th century overlanders journeying to the Northwest used to talk of "seeing the elephant, hearing the owl, and having gone to the other side of the mountain"—a colorful way of saying they had survived the difficulties and hardships of frontier life. While the Grange initially focused on taking the edge off the harshness of farm life through social and educational programs, it quickly became a major voice advocating rural free postal delivery, better farm-to-market transportation, improved marketing facilities, direct primary elections and the graduated income tax.

When citizens of Washington recall such projects as the Columbia River development, rural electrification, agricultural research or the Grange PUD power bill, they're recalling the benefits all of us have received from the progressive public service of the Washington State Grange. The Grange, which began in 1889, received a great infusion of energy in 1905 when C.B. Kegley of Whitman County became Washington State Grange master. It is a legacy of commitment to our community and region that still lives.

As Gus Norwood's book so vividly describes, it is a history of which we can all be proud.

—U.S. Rep. Thomas S. Foley
House Majority Leader

PREFACE

WASHINGTON GRANGERS CELEBRATE A CENTURY!

Because of the Grange, Washington is a better state in which to live and work. The Grange has served the well-being of rural people and of all Washingtonians and this is the main social, economic and political theme of this history.

The introduction explains the Grange idea and organization. The first two chapters discuss formation of the National Grange and its early achievements while the third chapter describes the state of Washington setting. Chapters four and five trace the early formation of Granges in Oregon and Washington. The balance covers periods of Grange history under the leadership of each state master during the first 100 years.

The Washington State Grange was organized on September 10, 1889. Two months later, on November 11, 1889, Washington Territory became the State of Washington and joined the Union. In the past 100 years the state and the Grange have grown up together.

The Grange provides opportunity for each individual Grange member to help determine public policy. As a grass-roots organization, the individual does count and can make a difference.

Further, the Grange has been a leadership training school for those in all walks of public life. Grangers serve in positions of public trust and many first learned of their individual potential for leadership when they served the Grange.

Early on, the Grange reached beyond a mere concern about farm issues to matters of broad public interest. Much of the reputation of the organization resulted from legislative efforts that affected every citizen of the state. The Grange has a wide range of interests and new subjects are always coming up. It has evolved into a broad, public interest organization.

Centennial celebrations are fun but they also raise questions about the uncertain future. What will happen in the next 100 years? What can we make happen? The Grange story needs to be told because the lessons of 100 years can help us to meet the challenges of the century ahead.

Any human endeavor gains from a sense of history. John F. Kennedy paraphrased Abraham Lincoln in saying, "Until you know where you have been, you don't know where you are going."

Throughout the ages people have learned too late that the death of a grandparent silenced a source of valuable information about the past. The Grange has decided to seek out and to adopt the lessons of history. The sense of history has long appeared in the carefully kept minutes of the meetings, the voluminous proceedings of state and national conventions, in *The Grange News,* and in books on Grange history.

The spark behind the writing of this history was struck by the State Grange delegates at their 1964 Wenatchee convention—the organization's 75th anniversary. The diamond jubilee celebration included a presentation by Rose Nelson, wife of the master, on the history of Washington Granges from 1873 until the State Grange was formed in 1889. Her talk led the delegates to authorize the formation of the State Grange Historical Committee.

This committee has a history of its own under the distinguished chairmanship of Jack Silvers, Adda Roberts, Helen Hodde, and since 1978 Frieda Berger. The 1984-1987 members included Margaret Manda, Vance Arter, Larry Walls, Frank McCartney, Avis Beam and Mabel Johnston.

The Historical Committee raised money, largely as memorials, to pay for a historical display case with sliding glass doors in the State Grange headquarters. Each Grange and Pomona was asked to appoint a historian or committee to write the local history and file a copy in the display case, which has a shelf of histories seven feet long. Selected Grange histories and picture albums were displayed each year in the history exhibit at the State Grange annual session. A pageant was put on to commemorate the U.S. Bicentennial in 1976. Meanwhile, Granges across the state have sent in treasures for this display case. What a great idea!

In recent years the committee began planning the writing of this history. They reproduced a set of the Oregon State Grange proceedings of 1873 to 1889 because for these 16 years Washington Granges reported to the Oregon State Grange. By 1980, the committee began outlining ideas for the history and established a file cabinet for historical materials. Since 1984, committee members have been helpful with advice on the writing of this book, reading and commenting on each chapter.

My knowledge of the Grange began in 1948. During an automobile ride, I listened as Clark County Grange Deputy Heye H. Meyer explained the role of the Grange in enacting the Grange Public Utility District (PUD) Power Bill in 1930. Today 29 PUDs operate electric or water utilities, some operate both and two operate a sewer service. Some operate large dams.

Heye H. Meyer (1885-1961) helped form Clark County PUD in 1938 and he served as PUD commissioner 23 years. With his encouragement I joined Minnehaha Grange No. 164 in 1948, transferring to Fishers No. 211 in 1977. Meyer was a director of Grange Insurance Association for 25 years and was on GIA's board of directors when he died.

Power issues often brought me in touch with each Washington State Grange master and other officers. When I was asked in 1984 to write the history of Washington Grangers, I accepted immediately. I could put my heart in this one.

For 40 years I have heard about or have seen the role of Grangers in the electric power battles of this state. In fact, I was so familiar with the Grange role in power that I had to bend over backward in order to be fair to the many other functions and activities of the more than 400 Granges of our state.

Like most Grangers, I believe in the things the Grange has advocated and fought for. It is a human story of hard work, great cost and perseverance against opposition and adversity. Predominantly, the Grange policy was advanced by practical approaches and dogged determination.

My thanks go to many people, the State Grange Historical Committee and the executive committee, our State Master Ray Hill and the State Grange headquarters staff. Past State Grange Secretary Frank McCartney let me take out the one and only copy of a lot of documents and provided valuable tables on membership, one of which is printed in the appendix.

I was so often impressed by the people with long memories. Besides Ray Hill, Frank McCartney, Jack Silvers and Frieda Berger, there were Avis Beam, Nita Berry, Mabel Johnston, Rolf Jemtegaard, Dan Jolly, Charlie Hodde, Olga Nelson, Kirby Billingsley, Dr. Wayne Rasmussen, Harriet Ann Crawford, Dr. Carlos Schwantes and Ira Shea.

Thank goodness for those who critically read and improved the writing. Special thanks go to Jack Silvers for factual corrections and handling of sensitive issues. He drank a lot of coffee at our house as he patiently went over each chapter. Margaret Elley Felt made helpful suggestions as did Lena R. Germann, Ken Billington and Vance Arter. Duane Shipman reviewed the facts on Grange Insurance Association. Avis Beam must have sent a hundred corrections. Another very special thanks to that good friend of the Grange and editor par excellence Russ Holt.

Washington State University faculty and staff extended every courtesy.

Easily the Chief Den Mother for this effort was Frieda Berger. Many others, including former National Master Ed Andersen, offered encouragement. So much teamwork recalls the 28-horse teams pulling the early wheat combine. Not least on this team was my wife Jean helping on editing in addition to putting each draft through the computer and making all the corrections. Thanks to all. Probably something still slipped through by way of error or need for improvement. Despite my good intentions, any shortcomings are mine.

Gus Norwood
Vancouver, Washington 1988

INTRODUCING YOUR LOCAL GRANGE

Neighbor is an old Anglo-Saxon word meaning a farmer living near you. Every American is fortunate indeed to have a farmer near at hand.

Likely this neighbor family belongs to the Grange. Members are known as Grangers. The state of Washington has more than 400 Granges in as many neighborhoods and a membership of more than 60,000 Grangers. The Washington State Grange is the largest state Grange in the nation, and as progressive as any in obtaining good legislation, good roads, rural mail service, good schools, rural electrification, Columbia River development and low cost power.

A self-portrait of the Grange appeared in the Golden Jubilee edition of *The Grange News* in 1939. Four pillars labeled legislation, cooperation, recreation and education were pictured. The strong emphasis on cooperatives could be seen from 1920 to the 1950s. Aside from steady growth of insurance and CENEX-Grange Supply, the Grange has more recently been less involved with cooperative business ventures.

The word Grange has a venerable history. It is best described in the 12-volume *English Oxford Dictionary* of 1933, as an establishment where farming is carried on; a country home with farm buildings attached including barns, stables, stalls, and other necessary places for husbandry. Chaucer in 1384 and Caxton in 1489 used the word in the sense of a granary or barn, one of the narrower meanings. Sicily was anciently the grange or breadbasket of the Romans. The *Oxford Dictionary* also notes that in 1867 in the United States the word was adopted as the name of an agricultural fraternal organization, the order of "Patrons of Husbandry."

By the end of the Civil War, farmers were in dire straits. The country was disrupted and in the Southern states the old system of plantation agriculture was destroyed. President Andrew Johnson asked the commissioner of agriculture to survey the situation and report on what could be done. He selected Oliver Hudson Kelley to make the survey. Kelley saw the need for a farm organization and, because of the breach between the North and the South, he felt it should be a fraternal organization. This led to formation of the Grange.

The founders of the Grange were familiar with the Masonic Order and sought a somewhat parallel fraternal organization structure and procedure, or ritual. In designing the ritual, the founders in 1867 borrowed from the English countryside of two centuries earlier. Each Grange was to have 16 officers.

The lords, dukes, earls or barons lived in their manors. The attached estate or farming operation was called the grange, and the owner was known as the master of the grange. In charge of operations was the overseer, much like a vice-president. The steward did the purchasing and had charge of tools and supplies. He had both men and women assistants. The chaplain was provided by the lord of the manor, as was the lecturer, or teacher. Many of the old estates were guarded by the gate keeper. All these titles as used on the English farms or granges were adopted in the Grange organization in the United States.

To ensure balanced representation for women in the Grange the founders provided the lady assistant steward and three titles from Roman mythology: Ceres, the goddess of grains; Pomona, the goddess of fruits; and Flora, the goddess of flowers. The usual panel of 16 officers of each Grange also includes a secretary, treasurer, and three members of the executive committee. In the Washington State Granges, however, since the late 1930s, there has been a 17th officer known as the chairman of women's activities. At the state level she is known as the director of women's activities.

In addition to carrying out the beautiful ritual and orderly procedures of the Grange, this array of officers serves useful purposes in providing opportunity for widespread participation by dividing the work, and for leadership training in each Grange.

With some modifications the pattern of officers is the same at the Pomona Grange, or county level, the State Grange and the National Grange.

The Grange ritual or meeting format uses seven degrees, each degree relating to both a farming activity such as sowing, cultivating, reaping and enjoying the harvest, and to the activity of the mind and the spirit, teaching the lessons of faith, hope, charity and fidelity. The local, or subordinate Grange observes four degrees corresponding to the four seasons. Pomona meets in the fifth degree, the state in the sixth, and national in the seventh degree.

The Granger cannot forget the admonition to cultivate the mind, as suggested by the symbolic use of seven farm implements:

"The Ax is used to cut away obstructions in the fields and to prepare timber for use. Its use teaches us perseverance in overcoming obstacles; for, as by repeated blows it cleaves its way through the hardest wood, so should we by repeated trials surmount every difficulty.

"The Plow is used to break up the ground and prepare it for planting. This should teach us to drive the plowshare of thought diligently through the heavy soil of ignorance, and thus prepare the mind for the growth of knowledge and wisdom.

"The Harrow is used to pulverize the soil as well as to cover the seed. Let this be emblematic of that course of study and observation necessary to enable you fully to understand your business.

"The Spade we use when we wish to penetrate deeper into the soil than we can with the Plow. It thus becomes the emblem of thoroughness. Whatsoever you attempt to do, strive to do it well.

"The Hoe, with which we cut up weeds, and stir the soil, is emblematic of that cultivation of the mind which destroys error and keeps our thoughts quickened and ready to receive and apply new facts as they appear, thus promoting the growth of knowledge and wisdom.

"The Pruning Knife, used to remove useless and injurious growth from our trees, plants and vines, should remind you to prune idle thoughts and sinful suggestions, and thus keep your passions within due bounds and prevent your fancy from leading you astray after the vanities and vices of the world. Bear in mind that moral and mental worth rank before worldly wealth or honor so that you can justly claim to belong to the true nobility of the land.

"The Sickle, like all tools we use, it is ancient and honorable; as an emblem of our Order, there is none more so. It speaks of peace and prosperity, and is the harbinger of joy. It is used not merely to reap the golden grain for the sheaf, but, in the field of mind and heart and soul, to gather every precious stalk, every opening flower, every desirable fruit.

"Thus shall the implement prove a reminder of honorable employment, preaching its sermon of present prosperity and peace, and its prophecy of future plenty and rejoicing."

Another important symbol is the agate:

"Let the Agate be to you an emblem of FIDELITY. May your principles of manhood and womanhood be as firmly impressed as the lasting colors in the stone, and may our friendship be as firm as the stone itself."

The cornucopia or Horn of Plenty is a final, all encompassing symbol that teaches sharing of the abundant gifts of the harvest.

The ritual includes an opening and closing prayer by the chaplain, and presentation of the flag. The Bible is placed on the altar and occasionally appropriate verses are read from it.

Some Grangers prefer less ritual and an abbreviated or short-form procedure is available for use as needed.

The quality of the Grange meeting depends mainly on the ability and effort of the lecturer to schedule interesting programs. The three goals of the lecturer are inspiration, education and amusement. While the business meeting may be very serious and involve debate, the lecturer must see to it that everyone has a good time. The Grange is a fun-loving organization.

The business meeting, usually monthly, considers committee reports and adopts motions or resolutions. This is what makes the Grange a grass-roots organization because this is where the resolutions originate. The resolutions calling for Grange action are passed on to Pomona, State or National, as appropriate. The week-long State Grange session involves the work of many committees, adoption of committee reports and resolutions, and election of officers.

Grangers love to sing and even recite poetry. An opening and closing song is normal but the program may include a sing-along or outside music and entertainment. Dances, formerly so prominent, are less likely to be sponsored by a Grange, but Grange halls continue to be widely used for dances, including use by square-dance clubs.

The Grange songbook reflects a history of change. Two songs that appeared in the songbook used between 1891 and 1925 illustrate the changing folklore. The song "Plow Deep's the Motto" has given way to the no-till or minimum-till methods of soil conservation. Another old song "Do Not Mortgage the Farm" reveals the pathos of wholesale farm foreclosures. As fashions changed and mortgages paid for $70,000 combines, the song disappeared, but because of the recent wave of farm foreclosures, many Grangers today might think it should be put back in the songbook.

CHAPTER ONE

1775 - 1873

EMBATTLED FARMERS FORM GRANGES

"By the rude bridge that arched the flood,
Their flag to April's breeze unfurled,
Here once the embattled farmers stood
And fired the shot heard round the world."

Concord Hymn, July 4, 1837
Dedication of Monument,
Ralph Waldo Emerson

Emerson's immortal words "the embattled farmers" did more than pay tribute to those who fell at Lexington and Concord on April 19, 1775. He provided a rallying cry for farmers, farm leaders and orators.

The embattled farmers overcame their traditional reluctance to band together. They did organize to better their lot. The Grange began in 1867 and was sweeping the country by 1873. The Grange was an American response of farmers and rural leaders to the problems facing agriculture.

Farmers have been embattled throughout the ages. Since time immemorial the nomadic hill people have raided the valley people. The farmers had helped to launch civilization by planting crops, developing tools, and domesticating animals. This made settlement possible and permitted development of the arts. But the success of farming made possible the military class living in their hilltop castles and for thousands of years ruling the peasants, especially in Europe. The discovery and settlement of America provided a way for the downtrodden peasants of Europe to find release. In America they sought freedom and peace.

Carving new farms out of the wilderness or "busting" the tough sod of the endless prairies did not provide an easy pathway to freedom or economic security. But it provided a way where none existed before.

During the two centuries since the Revolutionary War, American farmers have been embattled so many ways as to require a catalogue. The crops have suffered from the extremes of climate, from hot and cold, floods and drought, tornadoes, blizzards, hurricanes, dust storms, hail and lightning. The farmer had to share his crops with the birds, wild animals and insects. High freight costs, usurious interest rates, costly machinery, erratic market conditions and the exactions of middlemen have often resulted in a failure to break even, much less make a profit.

The public image of farming has ranged widely from the romanticists to the harsh reality of Millet and Markham. Jean Francois Millet (1814-1875) came of a peasant family and spent his youth working on his father's farm. He painted over a dozen masterpieces on the pathos of French peasant life: The Angelus, The Sowers, The Reapers, The Gleaners, and in 1863, The Man with the Hoe. The latter is now in a San Francisco art gallery. One who felt deeply about the painting was Edwin Markham (1852-1940) who was born in Oregon City, Oregon, and spent his boyhood in California as a farmer, blacksmith and cattle and sheepherder. In 1899, Markham published in the San Francisco Examiner his poem, "The Man with the Hoe." It was widely reprinted and it received much editorial comment.

> "Bowed by the weight of centuries he leans
> Upon his hoe and gazes on the ground."

Markham's poem raised a public cry of outrage that it had gone too far, but it did chill the idyllic view of the poets about the romance of farmers and farming.

One of America's great editors and a friend of the farmer, who understood farming conditions of his time, was Horace Greeley (1811-1872). As early as 1837, the year of Emerson's poem, he preached, "Go West, young man, go forth into the country." John Greenleaf Whittier hailed Greeley as our latter day Franklin mainly because of Greeley's lifelong interest in agriculture.

Explaining his advocacy of federal government measures to help farmers, Greeley said, "Not that they toil, but that they toil so hopelessly." He had no illusions about the romance of farming on the worn-out soil of the Eastern states, but saw better prospects west of the Appalachians. He knew whereof he spoke because his own sister was a victim of the daily round of farm drudgery.

Greeley founded the New York Tribune in 1840, helped form the New York Farmer's Club and set up the farm department at the Tribune with emphasis on reviewing farm books and reporting on farming conditions in the U.S. In 1860, as a liberal Republican member of the convention, he helped nominate Abraham Lincoln for president.

Greeley advocated land reform in 1846 and was elated by the passage of the Homestead Act of 1862. He feared the waning influence of agriculture and favored industrial-type universities to teach the agricultural sciences, an idea he pressed on Senator Justin Smith Morrill. Senator Morrill's first bill was passed in 1857, but was vetoed by President Buchanan. President Lincoln gave the bill his support and the Land-Grant College Act of 1862 has ever since been known as the Morrill Act. Greeley had pleaded since 1852 for a full-scale U.S. Department of Agriculture, but had to settle in 1862 for a department headed by a Commissioner of Agriculture.

Great Friends of the Farmer. Most of our presidents have recognized the need for a healthy farm economy. George Washington, Thomas Jefferson and Abraham Lincoln took the first important steps to help farmers.

George Washington (1732-1799) was most active as a planter at Mount Vernon, 1759 to 1775, and thereafter depended on an overseer to manage Mount Vernon and other lands totaling about 70,000 acres. His tobacco crop reached 89,000 pounds in 1763 but 10 years later was down to 5,000 pounds when he shifted to wheat. He began growing alfalfa in 1760, imported the Rotherham plow and grain drills, used mules, raised sheep, operated a dairy and carried on a large correspondence devoted mainly to agriculture.

In a farm manager, Washington demanded a man who was "...above all, Midas-like, one who can convert everything he touches into manure, as the first transmutation toward gold; in a word, one who can bring worn out and gullied lands into good tilth in the shortest time." President Washington's July 20, 1794, letter to the chairman of England's Agricultural Board, Sir John Sinclair, discussed the possibilities of agricultural societies: "I know of no pursuit in which more real and important service can be rendered to any country, than by improving its agriculture... It will be some time, I fear, before an Agricultural Society with Congressional aids will be established in this Country; —we must walk, as other countries have done, before we can run. Smaller Societies must prepare the way for greater, but with the light before us, I hope we shall not be so slow in maturation as older nations have been..." Washington's last annual message to Congress December 7, 1796, asked for general attention to the advancement of agriculture, commerce and manufactories, and asked for a Board of Agriculture, after the pattern then used in England.

Thomas Jefferson (1743-1826) applied his education to uproot unworthy traditions. His frontier was agricultural and practical. Monticello was operated as a progressive experimental farm where new machinery, new methods and crops were tested. He grew 32 vegetables and developed an all-metal plow with a mold board that effectively turned the soil. In addition, Jefferson designed a seed drill, a hemp brake and an improved threshing machine. Agriculture is a constantly recurring theme in his farm book, his garden book and at least 325 letters.

In his *Notes on Virginia* (1785) he says, "Those who labor in the earth are the chosen people of God, if ever He had a chosen people, whose breasts He has made His peculiar deposit for substantial and genuine virtue."

Agriculture was basic to Jefferson's philosophy of life. He wrote from Paris to John Jay, "Cultivators of the earth are the most valuable citizens. They are the most vigorous, the most independent, the most virtuous, and they are tied to their country, and wedded to its liberty and interests, by the most lasting bonds."

Jefferson's greatest contribution was helping to write the land laws of 1785 and 1787, and later, making land readily available to small farmers and other settlers. His acquisition of Louisiana Territory doubled the size of the nation.

Abraham Lincoln (1809-1865) wrote little about farming but succeeded in obtaining legislation of importance to farmers. His one farm speech was in Milwaukee on September 30, 1859, at the state fair sponsored by the Wisconsin State Agricultural Society. In that speech he noted the growth of agricultural fairs and their dual educational and recreational benefits. Fairs were praised for helping to exchange and disseminate new ideas. He urged study to achieve greater crop yield, discussed the application of steam power on the farm, and then encouraged the deeper study of agriculture to grow two blades of grass where there was but one before.

As president, he asked Congress in 1861 to create a Department of Agriculture. He signed the resulting law May 15, 1862, but it created only a Commissioner of Agriculture. Five days later he signed the Homestead Act, under which, in time, a million farms were created. The Land Grant College Act (Morrill Act), which Lincoln signed in 1862, led to formation of the agricultural colleges.

The Pacific Railroad Act of 1862 and the Northern Pacific Act of 1864 authorized large land grants to encourage transcontinental railways, helping to settle the Pacific Northwest.

In freeing the slaves by proclamation in 1863, Lincoln set in motion a constitutional amendment to abolish slavery in all states. This, and the war between the states, effectively abolished the plantation system, encouraging the family farm approach.

Finally, Lincoln often explained a decision to take some action by explaining the purpose for which the people created government: "The legitimate object of government is to do for the people what needs to be done, but which they cannot, by individual effort, do at all, or do so well, for themselves." President Lincoln appointed Isaac

Newton as the first Commissioner of Agriculture. But the preoccupation with the war between the states precluded much activity until after the war. Two of Newton's early appointments for the new Department of Agriculture soon became involved beyond the call of duty. They were William Saunders and Oliver Hudson Kelley, two of the founders of the National Grange.

Kelley Envisions Grange. Although Saunders was appointed several years earlier, the story of the origins of the National Grange begins properly with Kelley, who first envisioned the organization.

Oliver Hudson Kelley (1826-1913) was born in Boston and attended school there. He went to Chicago at 21 to work in a drugstore, then as a reporter for the Chicago Tribune and as a telegraph operator in Peoria and Muscatine. He married in 1849 and took up a claim at Itasca, Minnesota, on the Mississippi River to begin farming. He joined the Masons, becoming the first member in Minnesota. In 1851, his wife died at 19, leaving an infant daughter who died six months later.

On July 7, 1852, Kelley married Miss Temperance Baldwin Lane of Boston, then a teacher in Minnesota. They had four daughters. She

Oliver Hudson Kelley

was destined to become a powerful and helpful factor in her husband's future. A partial crop failure in 1864 led Kelley to go to Washington as a clerk in the Department of Agriculture for that winter, returning to his farm the next spring.

In October 1865, Commissioner Newton sent Kelley an urgent request to come to Washington. President Andrew Johnson wanted a survey made of agricultural conditions in the South as the basis for hastening rehabilitation of southern farming and as part of the post-Civil War reconstruction effort. The assignment went to Kelley.

Kelley started in January 1866, traveling through Virginia and North Carolina. He spent six weeks in Charleston, South Carolina, and then reported to the president in May. He had found his Masonic connection crucial in helping to overcome Southern resentment against Northerners. His mission had been delicate and required great tact.

During that spring of 1866 tour of the destitute conditions in Southern agriculture Kelley wrote Miss Caroline A. Hall, his wife's niece in Boston, on the need for a farm organization. In his book on the origins of the Grange written in 1875, Kelley explained that he was convinced that the politicians would "never restore peace in the country; if it came at all it must be through fraternity...to restore kindly feelings among the people." He mentioned in his book the reply of Miss Hall expressing "sympathy for the women of the South and strongly encouraged my suggestion that an organization of the farmers of the country might prove to be a blessing."

With his report to the president, Kelley's immediate mission was ended, and he returned to a belated season of farming. Always his mind was occupied with questions on how to form a farm organization. By now he knew it was as much needed in the North as in the South. Again he applied for a job in Washington, D.C., and received a better appointment as a clerk in the post office starting January 1867.

This provided him a chance to try out his idea on others and to recruit coworkers. The first two were John R. Thompson of the U.S. Treasury Department and William M. Ireland in the Post Office Department. Both were Masons. Reverend John Trimble, an Episcopalian in the Treasury Department, readily joined the group. Not so quick to join was William Saunders, an outstanding landscape architect who doubted the feasibility of a ritualistic fraternity. He agreed, however, to test the idea at the St. Louis meeting of a pomology (fruit grower) organization where he found strong acceptance. Two other recruits were Francis M. McDowell, a former banker who retired to a New York farm, and Universalist clergyman Reverend

A.B. Grosh, a worker in the Department of Agriculture.

These seven, destined to become the founders, met often in the office of William Saunders, Superintendent for the Propagating Gardens of the Department of Agriculture. They set up the constitution and the ritual, and prepared promotional material. Among the basic decisions made by the founders was to approve Kelley's suggestion of full and equal membership for women. Miss Caroline Hall had urged such equality with the admonition, "Your organization will never be permanent if you leave the women out."

The Grange is Born. Saunders had solicited advice from farm leaders he knew. One advised bringing in the youth, and this was done. The initiation fee was also adopted based on a suggestion. At the November 15, 1867, meeting the name "Patrons of Husbandry" was adopted as the name of the organization. The name "Grange" was adopted to designate the organizational units including the National Grange. The organization meeting—the birthday of the National Grange—was held on December 4, 1867. It formed the National Grange of the Patrons of Husbandry and officers were elected. William Saunders was elected as the first national master; Kelley was elected national secretary. On January 8, 1868, Potomac Grange No. 1 was formed in part to try out the ritual.

Saunders (1822-1900) was born in Scotland. Three paternal ancestors had been gardeners. He passed up an opportunity to pursue the ministry and instead served as an apprentice to a famous gardener and then studied horticulture at the University of Edinburgh. In 1848, he married and sailed for America, found work as a gardener on a private estate in Connecticut, then designed the landscaping for the Johns Hopkins estate. He became a nurseryman and developed the fixed glass roof for greenhouses. An authority on horticulture, he wrote much and served as an assistant editor of a horticultural publication. While it was Kelley who first envisioned the Grange, specifically, Saunders had advocated as early as 1855 that farmers organize in some effective way.

Commissioner Newton appointed Saunders as Superintendent of the Propagating Gardens in 1862 where he served 38 years until his death in 1900 at age 77. He designed the planting for the Mall in Washington D.C., planned the National Cemetery at Gettysburg, reviewed the plans with President Lincoln and on November 19, 1863, sat on the platform when Lincoln gave the Gettysburg Address.

In 1868, he imported the seedless navel orange from Brazil and introduced it in California with eminent success. He introduced and developed many plants and made many landscape plans.

He served as national master of the Grange December 1867 to January 1873, then three years on the executive committee. His great contribution to the Grange was his sound judgment which was often needed to guide the impulsive enthusiasm of Secretary Kelley.

Kelley's enthusiasm faced its most severe test in April 1868 as he launched his crusade to organize Granges. He quit his job and started with very little money, thinking that he would organize Granges and use the funds thus available. At Harrisburg he raised $15 but no Grange was formed. He then went to Fredonia, New York, the home of National Grange Assistant Steward A.S. Moss. He and Moss organized Fredonia Grange No. 1 on April 16, 1868. When he reached Madison, Wisconsin, Kelley had to borrow money for the train fare to get to his farm on May 1, utterly disheartened. Kelley felt the farmer was "not willing to help himself."

Temperance Kelley came to the rescue. Her husband did not know that she had just inherited a small legacy of $500. This she gave to her husband so he could resume his efforts. Kelley did resume and he did so in an adverse period of farm turbulence and transition.

The Civil War had triggered an energy revolution on American farms from hand power to horsepower. The war factors were mainly manpower shortages, rising demand for food and higher prices for farm produce. The rise of the steel industry and availability of recently invented horse-drawn farm equipment encouraged farm mechanization. For example, one Northern factory produced 30,000 horseshoes per day to provide an advantage the South did not have. The importance of horses was recognized by General Grant, a farmer himself, when at Appomattox he allowed the defeated Confederates to retain their horses as they would be needed "for the spring plowing."

Seven million immigrants entered the U.S. from 1837 to 1873 and many took farms. Easterners moved west to better land. Liberal land laws like the Homestead Act invited settlers. Extension of railroads in the Midwest opened the breadbasket of America for settlement. All this brought increased productivity and increased total agricultural production, but also a steady, unrelenting, heartbreaking decline in farm prices. Prices went down to where farmers could not pay the railroads for shipping the produce. This was the uneasy farm climate of 1868 to the financial panic of 1873.

For Kelley, 1868 turned out to be a vintage year. His morale went up when he learned that a Grange had been organized at Newton, Iowa, on April 17, 1868, a result of literature mailed out during 1867.

The biggest boost was the arrival of Mrs. Kelley's niece, Miss Caroline Hall, to become Kelley's assistant. Her experience as a

Oliver Hudson Kelley's 189-acre farm in Elk River, Minn., was purchased by the National Grange in 1935 and presented to the Minnesota Historical Society in 1961. It is a "living history" farm where farming practices of the mid-nineteenth century are displayed for the public.

Minnesota Historical Society photo

teacher proved helpful in keeping up the correspondence. Late in 1868, the National Grange appointed Miss Hall to the office of Ceres.

Kelley concentrated on organizing his home state. North Star Grange No. 1 at St. Paul was formed in the fall of 1868 and nearly a dozen Granges followed. The Minnesota State Grange was established in 1869 as the first state Grange. Iowa State Grange followed in 1871. Creation of temporary state organizations speeded up the work. In 1871, the Kelley family moved to Washington, D.C., and Miss Hall managed the office. By the close of 1872 there were 1,105 Granges.

Meanwhile, demands were increasing that the Grange should become active in legislation and cooperation. Kelley was receptive but another of the founders, McDowell, was more conservative because he feared moving too fast and because he felt that business ventures would not work.

The decision, however, would not be made by Kelley and McDowell. Iowa State Master Dudley W. Adams had both the vision and enthusiasm of Kelley and the cautious judgment of William

Saunders. At the fifth National Grange session in January 1872 Adams was elected national lecturer. That fall, in October 1872, Iowa State Master Adams addressed a large Iowa farm meeting to express the growing sentiment of unrest. As Grange historian Gardner reports the speech, Adams "broke loose."

"What we want is a new Declaration of Independence... We have heard enough, ten times enough, about the hardened hand of honest toil, the supreme glory of the sweating brow, and how magnificent is the suit of coarse homespun which covers a form bent with overwork...I tell you, my brother tillers of the soil, there is something in this world worth living for besides hard work. We have heard enough of the professional blarney about the honest farmer, the backbone of the nation... We have been too much alone. We must exchange views. Above all, we must think."

At the January 1873 National Grange session Adams was elected the second national master and served two years. This marked the shift in control from the original founders to the state masters. The session voted for the first time to print the proceedings. There were only 23 men and four women as voting delegates but they represented 11 state Granges. Mrs. Kelley entertained the members of the entire delegate body at her home.

The surge of Grange membership in 1873 was almost explosive. Buck's 1913 book, *The Granger Movement*, shows the number of Granges in each state or territory from 1873 to 1876. In 1874, Iowa led with 1,918 Granges. In February of that year, Adams' National Master's Address claimed a one-year national increase in Granges from 1,300 to 12,000. The record month of February 1874 brought in 2,239 new local Granges. The financial panic of 1873 undoubtedly helped to drive up the membership to its 1875 peak, but the failure of Grange business ventures brought sharp losses of membership in 1876.

Buck's book was not specifically a history of the National Grange of the Patrons of Husbandry, although he gave the Grange a prominent place. His book was generally about farmer unrest of 1870 to 1880 and the farmer legislative efforts of that time, notably to regulate the railroads.

Much of the farmer sponsored legislation was thrown out by the courts or had to be repealed, but one Illinois law passed muster in 1876. It prevailed. The Grange achieved a notable success before the highest court of the land.

CHAPTER TWO

1876-1890

THE GRANGE'S GREATEST VICTORY

"Every contract, combination in the form of trust or otherwise, or conspiracy, in restraint of trade or commerce among the several states, or with foreign nations, is hereby declared to be illegal."

Sherman Antitrust Act of 1890

The "Grange's greatest victory" are words of Judge Thurman Arnold, U.S. Court of Appeals, and from 1938 to 1943 head of the Antitrust Division of the U.S. Department of Justice and chief advisor to President Franklin Roosevelt on antitrust matters. Judge Arnold referred to the important United States Supreme Court decision in 1876 in the case of Munn v. Illinois, and the far-reaching, public interest benefits resulting from the decision. The decision opened the door for much progress in social and economic legislation, including the Sherman Antitrust Act of 1890.

The case involved one of the so-called Granger Laws sponsored by various farm groups to curtail the high rates and unfair practices of railroads and grain warehouse companies. The pressure for enacting the Granger Laws centered in Illinois and came from the Illinois State Grange, Illinois State Farmers' Association, a farmer-sponsored Producers Convention of early 1870, and *Prairie Farmer*, one of the oldest farm papers. Their first major impact was on the Illinois Constitutional Convention of 1870, which mandated regulation of railroads and grain elevators or warehouses. New laws of 1871 were revised in 1873 and remain on the books today. The farmers had gotten their act together in the form of carefully written laws. Farmers complained of excessive freight and storage charges, many forms of discrimination and bad service. Rates were higher for short hauls than for long hauls, and between points where there was no competition. Railways gave free passes to legislators, judges, and even Grangers going to a convention. The list of grievances went on and on.

Munn v. Illinois involved an 1871 Illinois law requiring grain warehouses and elevators to apply for a license and to charge no more than the rates specified in the law. The Munn warehouse refused to apply for a license, they overcharged, and upon complaint, the state hailed the firm into court and the court levied a $100 fine. The firm appealed, and the Illinois Supreme Court in 1873 upheld the law and the lower court decision. Upon further appeal, the U.S. Supreme Court upheld the law as constitutional in a landmark opinion. The U.S. Supreme Court on the same day applied its Munn v. Illinois opinion to a group of railroad cases in which it upheld the authority of state legislatures to regulate railroads.

Because the story was complex and little known, the National Grange in 1964 sponsored an essay contest for law school students on the subject, "Impact of the Grange on Social Legislation." Judge Arnold chaired the panel which selected the four winners. They were John C. Miles Jr., Robert S. Lingo, William E. Falck and Alfred B. Strand Jr. At the 100th annual session of the National Grange in Minneapolis on November 17, 1966, he presented the awards and made the presentation address.

The four essays and the presentation address stand out. They were printed by the National Grange in 1967 as a 100-page booklet, "Legal and Economic Influence of the Grange 1867-1967." It deserves an honored place on the Grange bookshelf. All four essays drew from Buck's *The Granger Movement* for the historic situation in 1870 to 1880 which led to farmer discontent, the Granger Laws, the Granger Cases and the keystone decision of 1876 in Munn v. Illinois. Each essay interpreted that decision as a turning point for government from a laissez faire policy or nonintervention in business, to an assertion of government sovereignty first at the state level and then federal, and the gradual use of governmental authority to regulate business for the common good.

While each essay uses a different style and approach, they are in general agreement in interpreting the longer term impact of Munn v. Illinois. They agree that the impact was modest at the time, resulting, however, in federal regulation of railroads after the enactment of the Interstate Commerce Act of 1887. From 1876 to 1934 the U.S. Supreme Court remained strongly pro-business and distrustful of the competence of state legislatures. In this period the U.S. Supreme Court interpreted Munn v. Illinois very strictly as applying only to regulation of public utilities. Only after the case of Nebbia v. New York (1934), which permitted regulation of wholesale and retail price of milk, did the Court concede to the legislatures the sovereign authority for "reasonable" regulation of business in the public interest.

Thus the long-term impact of the Granger Cases was not reached until after 1934. The Grangers in the 1870 decade and for much of the next century did not know and did not realize how well they had built. The publication of the booklet was a fitting, if belated, tribute to early Grangers and to the spontaneous, grass-roots movement in which free Americans reasserted their sovereignty through their representative governments. It was also a reassertion for the rule of law as against business monopoly. This is not to say that justice was certain and swift or that it had finally arrived. The last of the essays concluded, "I do not think that the Grange realized the impact it would have 100 years later. It has been felt on both the state and federal level and has brought regulations for the welfare of all the people, not just the farmer."

The logic used by the U.S. Supreme Court in 1876 changed the direction of American government. Chief Justice Morrison R. Waite based the majority opinion on a scholarly essay on the common law of England by Sir Mathew Hale, entitled, "Concerning Ports of the Sea," which discusses the obligations of the wharf or dock owner to his customers. The key paragraph from Waite's opinion reads in part:

"Looking then, to the common law, from whence came the right which the Constitution protects, we find that when private property is 'affected with a public interest it ceases to be *juris privati* only.' This was said by Lord Chief Justice Hale more than two hundred years ago, in his treatise *Di Portibus Maris*. (1 Harg. Law Tracts, 78) and has been accepted without objection as an essential element in the law of property ever since. Property does become clothed with a public interest when used in a manner to make it of public consequence, and affect the community at large. When, therefore, one devotes his property to a use in which the public has an interest, he, in effect, grants to the public an interest in that use, and must submit to be controlled by the public for the common good, to the extent of the interest he has thus created. He may withdraw his grant by discontinuing the use; but so long as he maintains the use, he must submit to the control..."

The Munn v. Illinois decision was for a long time regarded as great because it was the legal foundation for state regulation of public utilities. That in itself was a big step forward. This assumption also meant that the decision did not apply to any other businesses except public utilities. But in time the opinion was reread and studied and it became apparent that Chief Justice Waite had left the door open to state legislatures to address any general area of public concern and provide for reasonable regulation for the common good. The four law student essays provided many examples that go far beyond the public utility fields to include civil rights, hours and wages of employees, sale of alcohol, child labor and many fields of social legislation. If the state legislature saw that there was a public need, it could legislate to serve or alleviate that need.

Sherman Antitrust Act. Since the four essays would be printed, Judge Thurman Arnold commended them to the Grange and then devoted his presentation address to another subject. He commended and thanked the Grange for its role in making possible the enactment by the Congress of the Sherman Antitrust Act of 1890. It states simply, "Every contract, combination in the form of trust or otherwise, or conspiracy, in restraint of trade or commerce among the several states, or with foreign nations, is hereby declared to be illegal."

The law was very much needed because trusts were springing up in many industrial and commercial lines of endeavor. The Standard Oil Company, U.S. Steel, General Electric Company and the American Telephone and Telegraph Company were examples of fields in which competition had been sharply reduced, control of market established and prices increased. However, no president before Theodore Roosevelt ventured to use the new law.

Theodore Roosevelt became president just at the time that J.P. Morgan and E.H. Harriman were planning to merge two competing railroads, the Northern Pacific and the Great Northern, under the Northern Securities Company. President Theodore Roosevelt, a longtime student of monopoly, decided to move. He saw the issue as nothing less than effective national sovereignty. Big business was rapidly becoming the real sovereign. In 1904, the U.S. Supreme Court ruled 5 to 4 for the government, and stopped the merger.

The Twilight Zone. Theodore Roosevelt often referred to the efforts of companies to escape regulation. In the James River Veto of January 15, 1909, he said, "...the great corporations are acting with foresight, singleness of purpose and vigor to control the water powers of the country. They pay no attention to state boundaries and are not interested in the constitutional law affecting navigable streams except as it affords what has aptly been called 'a twilight zone' where they may find a convenient refuge from any regulation whatever by the public, whether through the national or the state governments."

The "twilight zone" for jurisdiction over U.S. railroads was created in 1886 in the case of Wabash, St. Louis, and Pacific Railway v. Illinois. The Supreme Court said that no state can exercise any control over commerce which passes beyond its limits. The Grange called for federal regulation of railroads.

Congress had started its studies of the complaints against railroads almost 20 years earlier in 1867, but railroad friends, particularly in the U.S. Senate, saw no urgent need for federal regulation, and a Maryland senator in 1873 declared that it would clearly be unconstitutional. Full scale investigations got under way in 1873 spurred by the explosive growth of the Grange and numerous petitions from state legislatures. The pressure for action diminished when the Court decided Munn v. Illinois in 1876 to allow state regulation of interstate commerce until such time as the Congress acts. This is the part of the Munn decision that fell by the wayside in 1886 with the Wabash case. Another spur for federal action was the periodic suggestion that railroads should be publicly owned, and that canals should be built to provide competition.

Interstate Commerce Act. National Grange Master Dudley W. Adams of Iowa devoted the Master's Address in February 1874 in St. Louis to the railroad problem and the need for action by Congress. "I see no solution of this question but for Congress to avail itself of its constitutional right to regulate commerce between the states," he said, "and for the states themselves to regulate the tariffs

Construction of railroads brought mixed blessings to farmers in the Northwest. Below, a Northern Pacific track laying crew reaches the Mosquito Creek Bridge high in the Cascades in 1886.

University of Washington Library photo, Special Collections Div., Negative 274

within their own boundaries... To rely on competition for relief will bring only renewed disappointment. Our past history shows that the rapid increase of railroads has only resulted in more gigantic combinations."

National Grange membership declined sharply in the last half of the 1870s but stabilized in the 100,000 to 200,000 range for the rest of that century. Meanwhile, other farm groups, merchants and other shippers helped put pressure on Congress.

The Interstate Commerce Act, as passed in February 1887, declared that charges must be reasonable and just. It prohibited rebates, drawbacks, the long-and-short-haul evil and monopolistic pools. The Interstate Commerce Commission, however, was not given authority to fix rates. If the ICC considered rates too high, the burden of proof was on the ICC. The view of the railroads was reflected in the fact that the price of railroad stocks rose when the act was passed. The investor clearly benefited from the ICC law together with big users of railway service. The ICC uniform system of accounts facilitated auditing and more honest accounting. Second, the Interstate Commerce Act provided standards and ground rules for all states and it provided an assurance of stability and continuity for the rules of the game.

Grangers did not get everything they wanted, but viewed the act as a step in the right direction. It put an end to the more obvious evils. Much later, of course, the act became a precedent for other federal regulatory legislation.

Far-Reaching Influence. The Grange had fought the battle for both state and federal legislation. Because both federal and state regulation were needed, Judge Arnold doubly commended the Grange for influencing both state and federal legislation that was far-reaching.

Another compliment came from Frederic A. Johnson in an article in the New York Law Journal in 1962.

"The Grange has earned its indisputable place as the foremost champion of the rights to private property through its exclusive advocacy, in the first instance, and from its undeviating support, thereafter, of the judicial postulate that subjects to reasonable governmental regulation the incidences of corporate or individual ownership whenever either is found to poach upon the area of public welfare."

The Grange at the time of the Munn v. Illinois decision in 1876 was only nine years old. The Grange's greatest victory was a victory for all Americans.

CHAPTER THREE

1825 - 1846

THE FIRST FARM IN WASHINGTON

"It was not farming and fur trading per se that clashed; rather, it was the freehold farm and the company's monopoly."

James R. Gibson

George Washington had been president three years when Captain Robert Gray entered the Columbia River on May 12, 1792. Gray named the river after his ship and established the earliest basis for the U.S. claim to the area now called the state of Washington.

Farming began in the area in 1825, long before it officially became a state. It was admitted to the Union as the 42nd state on November 11, 1889, but prior to admission, for 36 years from 1853, it had been known as Washington Territory. In 1853, Congress considered calling it Columbia Territory but amended the bill to name it Washington. From 1848 for five years, the area was officially part of Oregon Territory, that vast area from the Rocky Mountains to the Pacific Ocean between the 42nd and 49th parallels—that is, between the California and British Columbia boundaries. The congressional decision to create the Oregon Territory in 1848 was a result of the massacre of Marcus and Narcissa Whitman and 12 others near Walla Walla in November 1847 by Cayuse Indians. Oregon became the 33rd state in 1859.

Before the Oregon Treaty of 1846, which set the present boundary with Canada, Washington had two names. The Hudson's Bay Company considered that its Department of the Columbia extended to Spanish California while the United States claimed that its Oregon Country extended to Russian Alaska. The Treaty of Joint Occupation of 1818 permitted nationals of both the United States and Great Britain to live in the disputed area.

Since its chartering in 1670, the Hudson's Bay Company had been an important arm of British policy. From 1825 to 1846 the company established the first farm in the region and used farming as a tool of economic control and diplomatic persuasion. It worked hard to ensure that Washington west and north of the Columbia River would always be British. The failure of the first farm was a factor in settling the boundary dispute because the Hudson's Bay Company no longer

Agriculture in the Pacific Northwest got its start at forts operated by the Hudson's Bay Company. Farms at early Fort Vancouver, above, supplied food for permanent residents at the outpost.

National Archives photo courtesy of National Park Service

had a compelling economic interest and incentive in the region. The fur trade had declined and agriculture had lost its profitability. The first farm had provided two lessons. The company learned what to grow and where. In the end, however, the Hudson's Bay Company farms failed because even the company employees preferred the family farm approach on land of their own as against corporation farming.

The boundary dispute began in 1792. In that year, both Robert Gray for the United States and George Vancouver for Great Britain claimed the Columbia River country. After agreeing to the Treaty of Joint Occupation of 1818, the British Government decided to strengthen its claim to the area north of the Columbia River. The two major fur companies were both losing money. Sir Alexander Mackenzie had recommended that the Hudson's Bay Company and the

North West Company be merged. Parliament forced the merger in 1821, renewed the Hudson's Bay Company license for 21 years and granted it a monopoly on trading with the Indians west of the Rockies in addition to the monopoly already enjoyed within Canada east of the Rockies. The value of Hudson's Bay Company stock doubled. The company appointed George Simpson (1792-1860) as governor to reorganize the field operations on a profitable basis.

Fur traders obtained provisions three ways. Hudson's Bay Company ships brought stores from England to York Factory located where the Nelson River flows into Hudson Bay. Moreover, Bay traders minimized travel by persuading Indians to bring furs to company forts.

The North West Company out of Montreal established a pemmican factory on the Red River of the North. Pemmican consists of

Sir George Simpson
Nationaal Park Service photo

dried lean meat pounded into a paste with fat and preserved as pressed cakes. The Nor'Westers used pemmican based on buffalo meat plus supplies from the Indians to outflank the Bay traders and to reach the Pacific Ocean. After the merger, both provisioning methods were available to the enlarged operation.

In contrast, American fur traders lived off the land and sometimes obtained food from Indians, much as Lewis and Clark had done during their 1804-1806 adventure.

Governor Simpson in 1822 noticed the excellent gardens at Cumberland House on the Saskatchewan River. This set him to thinking about encouraging a policy of agricultural self-sufficiency at the forts west of the Rockies by means of farms.

There was another reason for the idea of fort gardens. On his three Pacific Ocean voyages Captain James Cook (1728-1779) had solved the problem of scurvy by emphasizing green vegetables in the diet as one means to overcome what later became recognized as deficiency of vitamin C. Ships carried barrels of sauerkraut, spruce beer and condensed beer.

Scurvy had become common in northern Canada during the long winters, hence the company encouraged the growing of cabbage and potatoes. Even York factory on the chilly shore of Hudson Bay had a cabbage patch. The countries of northern Europe had long recognized the nutritional values of cabbage in making cabbage soup and borsch. Borsch was also made with beets, another valuable source of vitamin C.

In 1824, Simpson and Dr. John McLoughlin left York Factory for the Columbia River. Everywhere they found inefficiency and poor management. In coming down the river, the Simpson-McLoughlin party camped at a place called Belle Vue Point or Jolie Prairie, present location of Vancouver, Washington. The place impressed the party as an excellent site and soon received much discussion. The party reached Fort George (Astoria) on November 8, 1824, and Simpson wintered there until March, meanwhile sending extensive reports to London.

Early in 1824, the British Foreign Office had suggested that the Hudson's Bay Company locate its facilities north of the Columbia River. Simpson decided to abandon Fort George as the headquarters but to retain it as a minor station. He felt the new headquarters should be at the mouth of the Frazer River, and he sent a party to explore the area that winter. Dr. John McLoughlin argued for locating the headquarters at Vancouver. Both sites won. Simpson, although worried about the sandbar at the mouth of the Columbia, designated the proposed Fort Vancouver as the new center but contemplated the Fort Langley site on the lower Fraser River as a future center. McLoughlin commenced building at Fort Vancouver late in 1824.

Simpson's diary records that on New Year's Day of 1825 Fort George, despite poor soil, had radishes, peas and carrots growing. There was no frost or snow. The climate was mild, but any future farm would be limited to 15 or 20 acres. In contrast, the Fort Vancouver site consisted of several thousand acres of extensive prairies ready for the plow. Simpson was no longer thinking of tiny garden patches. He praised the Jolie Prairie or Belle Vue Point in his report to the Committee in London:

"The place we have selected is beautiful as may be inferred from its Name and the Country so open that from the Establishment there is good travelling on Horseback to any part of the interior; a Farm to any extent may be made there, the pasture is good and innumerable herds of Swine can fatten so as to be fit for the Knife merely on nutricious Roots that are found here in any quantity and the Climate so fine that Indian Corn and other Grain cannot fail of thriving; it is much better than that of the Coast say at Point George being less exposed to the Sea Air."

On his return trip, Simpson inspected the partially built Fort Vancouver on March 18. The next morning he dedicated the place by breaking a bottle of rum on the flagstaff, and by 9 a.m. was headed upriver. In his diary report Simpson added to his praise:

"It will in Two Years hence be the finest place in North America, indeed I have rarely seen a Gentlemen's Seat in England possessing so many natural advantages and where ornament and use are so agreeably combined."

He also explained that the Vancouver name was used to "identify our claim to the Soil and Trade with his discovery of the River and Coast on behalf of Gt. Britain."

He delivered 10 bushels of seed potatoes to Fort Nez Perce, located where the Walla Walla River flows into the Columbia. He was making sure that every fort was getting the word to become self-sufficient by pursuing farming.

He found that Spokane House depended on five or six costly provisioning trips per year, and he complained that they were "eating Gold." He ordered its relocation to Kettle Falls where fish were plentiful and the bench along the river provided good farm land. He named the new station Fort Colvile, not to be confused with Colville, the Stevens County seat. Six bushels of potatoes from Spokane House were promptly planted.

Fort Colvile soon had two substantial farms capable of supplying potatoes and other provisions to the interior stations.

Plowing had started at Fort Vancouver April 21, 1825, and 100 bushels of seed potatoes were planted. That year the crop was 900 barrels of potatoes. By 1828 Vancouver had 153 cattle, not counting calves, 50 goats, 200 hogs and had harvested 400 bushels of corn, 1,300 wheat, 100 barley, 300 peas, 100 oats and 4,000 bushels of potatoes. Vancouver acreage reached 120 in 1829, 900 by 1837 and 1,420 in 1846. Four dairies were located on Sauvies Island. Fruit trees, berries, hops, grapes and a wide variety of vegetables also were grown. The two Colvile farms grew to 20 acres by 1827, 80 in 1833 and 200 in 1836 when over 5,000 bushels of grain were produced. By 1829 Colvile was known as the granary for the interior. It had a grist mill at Mill Creek, a dairy, large potato storage and a variety of livestock and vegetables. It went into decline in 1841.

Fort Langley was founded in 1827 for serving the northern posts. By 1840 the farm included 240 acres in crops, 240 cattle, 18 horses and 250 pigs, but the main operation was packing barrels of salmon for Hawaii.

The success of the company farms at Vancouver, Colvile and Langley enabled Simpson to reduce the provisioning trips and number of people involved in transport. In 1828, Simpson found agriculture to be the "main spring of the business." The payroll was cut in half and the company paid 10 percent dividends annually 1825-1840. Personnel were better employed around the year. Both Simpson and McLoughlin as early as 1832 foresaw eventual decline of the fur trade. In fact, Simpson adopted a policy of trapping out the beaver just west of the Rockies as a way of discouraging American trappers. Simpson saw in agriculture an opportunity to develop an export trade as a way of maintaining the strong monopoly position of the company in the Oregon Country.

The 1830s brought two significant changes. People began coming on the Oregon Trail. Jason Lee in 1834 arrived to set up a mission, and McLoughlin persuaded him to settle in Oregon, south of the Columbia. The Whitmans and Spaldings arrived in 1836 at Vancouver and established missions at Waiilatpu (near present Walla Walla) and Lapwai (near Lewiston, Idaho). The chief effect of the missionaries was to increase interest in migrating to the Oregon Country, beginning in 1840 and with a large surge in 1843 that was repeated each year in the decade following. McLoughlin funnelled almost all of the immigrants into the Willamette Valley.

The other significant development of the early 1830s was the

Dr. John McLoughlin
Oregon Historical Society photo, negative 245

decimation of the Indians in the lower Columbia River area by disease, believed to have been malaria brought in by ship. Entire tribes were wiped out. The new immigrants found no Indians to resist their settling.

On February 6, 1839, the Wrangell-Simpson Accord was signed at Hamburg, Germany, effective June 1, 1840, for 10 years. The Hudson's Bay Company was to supply the Russian American Company with agricultural produce, mainly 4,200 bushels of wheat in 1840 and thereafter 8,400 bushels each year plus flour, barley, peas, beef and ham. In turn, the Bay company would receive furs.

In 1839, Simpson and McLoughlin established the Puget Sound Agricultural Company as a subsidiary. They selected the Cowlitz Portage as the location, with a farm at each end. The Cowlitz farm at Cowlitz Prairie consisted of four square miles of mostly arable land just northeast of the present town of Toledo. Wheat was the main crop.

The Nisqually farm west of present day Tacoma was established 1840-1841 as the pastoral arm for livestock. It contained about 140 square miles of prairies lying east and north of the Nisqually River. From 1841 to 1846 the livestock population increased from 2,342 to 10,578 sheep, from 649 to 3,063 cattle and from 12 horses to 343.

In his excellent 1985 book *Farming the Frontier,* Professor James R. Gibson summarizes the status of the 23 Bay farming locations as of 1845 with cultivated acreage of 3,005. Livestock totaled 8,848 sheep, 4,430 cattle, 1,716 horses and 1,906 pigs.

West of the Rockies the Hudson's Bay Company had 23 forts, each with a farm, but they were operated as one farm and were eminently successful in ensuring the company's self-sufficiency. In order to meet the needs of the Russian American Company, however, the Hudson's Bay Company purchased considerable wheat in the Willamette Valley. Fluctuations in production were also taken care of by storage of grain and flour. Surplus flour was sold in Hawaii.

The failure of the Puget Sound Agricultural Company was caused by shortages of personnel. The recruitment of French-native farmers from the Red River of the North proved ineffective because, after a short time at Nisqually or Cowlitz, the new people would desert for better opportunities in the Willamette Valley. The people preferred to own their land and to farm their own land. The desertions of 1842 and 1843 discouraged further recruiting. The Bay farms were profitable from 1844 to 1849. Losses from 1850 and later resulted in abandonment of the Cowlitz farm in 1855. Nisqually became inoperative for a host of reasons centering on lack of personnel. Squatters moved in and they shot livestock. Indians rustled stock.

Fort Vancouver, headquarters for the Hudson's Bay Company in the region later known as both Oregon and Washington Territories, enjoyed an active trading business for many years. The facility is now a National Historic Site.
Library of Congress photo courtesy of the National Park Service

Indian dogs and wolves did much damage. One shepherd killed 100 wolves at Nisqually. Eagles killed lambs and one unknown disease killed 500 sheep. Drought, frost and forest and prairie fires added to the disruption. Much of the Nisqually farm is now in the Army's Fort Lewis.

The Oregon Treaty of 1846 settled the longstanding boundary dispute. The boundary was fixed at the 49th parallel and ensured U.S. ownership and jurisdiction over western and central Washington. The failure of the Hudson's Bay Company farming venture was a factor in that it left Great Britain with little immediate economic incentive to continue its claim to the disputed territory.

Simpson in 1842 had authorized McLoughlin to build Fort Victoria on Vancouver Island as part of a contingency plan, and this was done in 1843. Four large farms were platted at Fort Victoria. The headquarters was moved from Fort Vancouver to Fort Victoria in 1845 to 1849. By that time Simpson placed blame for Britain's loss of the Oregon Territory on McLoughlin for aiding the American immigrants and lending them credit. McLoughlin left Hudson's Bay Company, settled at Oregon City and became an American citizen, but was again badly treated.

The Treaty allowed for negotiations for the U.S. to acquire the Hudson's Bay Company properties. The request for $5.5 million was settled for $650,000 and was finally paid in 1869 and 1870.

Chief Factor James Douglas had warned in 1838 that "the interests of the (Willamette) Colony, and Fur Trade will never harmonize, the former can flourish, only, through the protection of equal laws, the influence of free trade, the accession of respectable inhabitants; in short by establishing a new order of things, while the fur trade, must suffer by each innovation."

Gibson's book concludes, "It was not farming and fur trading per se that clashed; rather, it was the freehold farm and the company's monopoly." For a brief historic period in the 1840s the Oregon country witnessed two systems or methods of farming. The corporation farm appeared to have large advantages but it could not compete against the desire of human beings to own and farm their own land.

Washington Becomes A Territory. The U.S. Congress did virtually nothing about providing a government for the Oregon country as a result of the 1846 treaty. The Hudson's Bay Company had started its gradual retirement to Vancouver Island in 1843, but did not sell the last of its property in the U.S. until about 1870. American settlers began staking claims north of the Columbia River as soon as the treaty was signed.

New settlements stopped almost as suddenly in 1847. The Hudson's Bay Company people had warned Marcus Whitman in 1846 and 1847 that the Indians might attack. On November 29, 1847, the Cayuse Indians murdered Marcus and Narcissa Whitman and 12 others and took a large party of hostages. Peter Skene Ogden of the Hudson's Bay Company ransomed the hostages.

The reports of the Whitman Massacre spurred the U.S. Congress. The Act of August 13, 1848, established the area west of the Rockies and between 42 and 49 degrees latitude as the Oregon Territory, and provided a governor and marshal. Governor Joseph Lane took over at Oregon City March 2, 1849. His census at that time showed only 304 settlers north of the Columbia River. Also in 1849, the U.S. Army established what was later named Vancouver Barracks.

The need for lumber in California soon stimulated the establishment of sawmills in the Puget Sound area. These settlers were not satisfied with the Oregon Territory government in remote Oregon City. When it was moved even farther to Salem, Oregon, the Puget Sound people looked for an alternative.

The Monticello convention of November 25, 1852, petitioned Congress to establish the Territory of Columbia. But by that time former Governor Lane had become Oregon Territorial Delegate and had introduced a bill to the same effect. The bill was amended to change the name of Columbia to Washington. The Territory of Washington was created by the Act of March 2, 1853, to include the area west of the Rockies and north of the Columbia River and 46 degrees north latitude and all of present-day Idaho.

An 1839 West Point graduate, Major Isaac I. Stevens, was appointed the first governor of Washington Territory and given two other assignments. As Superintendent of Indian Affairs he would negotiate treaties for acquiring Indian lands. Enroute to his post he would also survey a route for a railroad, a route later used by the Northern Pacific Railroad as authorized in 1864. His detailed report was published by Congress.

As a result of the Whitman Massacre and a decade of Indian wars the Army discouraged settlement east of the Cascade Mountains. The gold miners nonetheless went to the Orofino, Idaho, fields and provided a market for farm produce from the Walla Walla area. This helped to rebuild the Walla Walla area. The Idaho miners succeeded in persuading Congress in 1863 to establish the Territory of Idaho. The people in Walla Walla County, feeling very remote from Olympia, tried in 1876 to persuade Congress to permit them to annex to Oregon, which had become a state in 1859. In the 1870 census Walla Walla was the largest city in Washington Territory, having 5,300 people in its area compared to King County, including Seattle, with only 2,210 people.

Despite railroad surveys to Puget Sound, the first transcontinental railroad went to San Francisco with completion in 1869. It was called the Pacific Railroad but was made up of the Union Pacific and the Central Pacific railways. Settlers for the Pacific Northwest could take the train to San Francisco and a lumber boat to the Puget Sound. That did not bring many settlers and the census of 1870 showed the population of California at 560,247, Oregon 90,923 and Washington only 23,955.

CHAPTER FOUR

1873 - 1889

OREGONIANS FIGHT MONOPOLY

"...with every bushel of wheat the farmer sends away, he must send a bushel and a half more to pay its way. We sincerely hope the efforts of the farmers to secure cooperative action may meet with such success as will accomplish the desired results."
The Oregonian, February 1, 1873

When farmers get mad enough, they will organize. They had been mad for some time and had formed some farmers clubs. In time these became Granges. In the early years of the Grange in the Northwest, Washington and Idaho Granges were part of the Oregon State Grange. Washington Granges were not to have their own state Grange until 1889.

Oregon and Washington farmers were at the mercy of the Oregon Steam Navigation Company which enjoyed a monopoly on the Columbia River as well as substantial control and domination on the Willamette River.

In 1870, Oregon was well settled with 90,923 people and had been a state for 11 years. Washington was sparsely settled with only 23,955 people and would not be a state for 19 years. Hence, Washington farmers looked to Oregon for leadership in fighting the shipping monopolies.

Grange Comes to the West Coast. It is hard to imagine and difficult to believe that one man in the summer of 1873, given the transportation and communications difficulties of the time, could organize the California State Grange, the Oregon State Grange and, for good measure, launch Granges in Washington Territory. He had luck, he had help, but credit and praise are due N.W. Garrettson of Iowa for helping the Grangers of the West Coast.

Several things are hard to believe about the events from 1873 to 1889, a period of hard times. First, there was the spectacular membership growth of the Grange. Second, there were the business ventures undertaken by Granges. After brief success, these generally failed, and membership plummeted. Third, the farmers battled against navigation monopolies on the Willamette and Columbia Rivers. Eventually these efforts evolved into broad, multiple-purpose river basin development.

California in the 1870s was a significant wheat-growing state, selling surpluses in the Liverpool, England, market. The extortions of a ring of middlemen spurred California farmers in December 1871 to meet in Sacramento to form a farmers' club. Other clubs followed and in September 1872 the clubs united as the California Farmers' Union. The union launched several business enterprises including one for joint purchasing of grain sacks. News of the "secret" plan leaked out and the plan failed. Next year in April, 1873, National Grange deputy W.H. Baxter addressed the Farmers' Union convention at San Francisco, emphasizing the "more secret form of organization" of the Grange. He convinced them to reorganize as Granges. Thereupon the National Grange sent special deputy N.W. Garrettson to California. Forming a state Grange would require the organization of 15 subordinate Granges. By July 15, 1873, he and others had 35 Granges qualified, and on that date Garrettson organized the California State Grange at Napa.

Garrettson then proceeded to Oregon where he found many Granges already formed. Oregon farmers as early as 1853 had formed farmers' clubs. Initially one in Yamhill County sponsored an agricultural library. Some put on fairs and later merged in 1860 as the Oregon State Agricultural Society, which in 1861 held the first Oregon State Fair. Most farmers' clubs, however, tended to be more militant.

"The immediate cause of the formation of these clubs in Oregon was due to an outburst of indignation throughout the Willamette Valley against monopolies controlling transportation on the Columbia and Willamette Rivers," according to Edna A. Scott in her 1923 thesis "The Grange Movement in Oregon 1873-1900."

The February 1, 1873, Portland *Oregonian* commented in its editorial, "Oppressions and extortions of the railroad monopoly have been carried to such extents that farmers, the principal sufferers, are organized for resistance... They have not awakened too soon to the importance of taking some steps for protection. They now pay the railroads more than three times what it costs to transport grain the same distance on short lines of railroads in the Atlantic States."

In his history of the Oregon State Grange, Ben Buisman provided many quotations on the evils of the railroad and navigation monopolies, and then explained, "This was the fertile field which the

Navigation of the Columbia River was of interest to Grange members in both Oregon and Washington during the nineteenth century.

Dave Howard photo

Grange movement found when it came to Oregon in December of 1872."

He credits W.J. Campbell, a farmer from East Portland, with organizing Oregon's first Grange, Marshfield No. 1 (now Clackamas) on December 14, 1872. It was a 15-month effort during which Campbell corresponded with National Secretary Kelley. Kelley's letters gave Campbell much "leeway" in bending the rules. Campbell assisted in organizing at least 27 Granges in Oregon. In 1873, Garrettson and two deputies from California assisted in Oregon and included a 400-mile round trip to the Walla Walla area in Washington Territory to organize five Granges there.

Garrettson organized the Oregon State Grange at Salem, September 24-27, 1873. When Garrettson put a stop to any further "leeway" in applying the National Grange bylaws, Campbell took a walk. He remained a Granger but not active. Garrettson was embarrassed by the incident and made clear his respect for Campbell's dedication and effective work. The Oregon State Grange began with 40 Granges in Oregon and five in Washington Territory. The session elected a highly respected progressive farmer, Daniel Clark, as the first master. Two 1873 resolutions put the Oregon State Grange on record in favor of concrete objectives. First, the delegates voted for federal appropriations for improving the Willamette and Columbia rivers for navigation by building locks and removing obstructions. Second, they voted for establishing a cooperative system of trade both for buying and selling.

A major depression had begun for American farmers in 1870. The financial panic of September 1873 then additionally brought on six years of hard times for the entire economy. Farmers felt something was very wrong about the workings of the economy, and especially they felt strongly about the high cost of transporting and storing grain.

The founders of the Grange had in mind the social and intellectual objectives of the Grange, but the new members were hurting economically. Nationally the Grange quadrupled from 5,000 Granges in 1873 to over 21,000 at the start of 1875. The membership was estimated at over 800,000 at the peak. In Oregon the number of Granges increased from 37 in 1873 to 190 on July 1, 1876. The Oregon membership peaked at 10,885 members in 1875, a number not again reached in 50 years. It plummeted to a low of 1,440 in 1881. Washington Territory had five Granges in 1873, and 68 in 1876, but Washington membership peaked at 2,169 Grangers on October 1, 1875. The bubble didn't burst, it just went down almost as fast as it had gone up.

Number of Granges and Membership

	U.S.	Calif.	Oregon	W. T.*	Id. T.*
Aug. 2, 1873	5,062	35	12	0	0
Oct. 18, 1873	7,325	91	37	5	0
Mar. 1, 1874	14,365	156	112	19	2
Jan. 1, 1875	21,697	240	177	63	15
Oct. 1, 1875	19,007	263	186	66	16
July 1, 1876	15,127	173	190	68	15
		Membership			
Oct. 1, 1875	758,767	14,228	8,233	2,169	390
July 1, 1876	588,525	9,965	8,544	1,963	378

Source: Buck, The Granger Movement
*W.T., I.T.: Washington and Idaho Territories

A factor in the Oregon decline was the failure of the Grange-sponsored, but loosely-organized, agency system of selling wheat and buying wagons and farm machinery. Some short-term benefits were achieved but before long the rising debts terminated the operations and the remaining Grangers gradually paid off the debt. Many dropped out for fear they might be liable. This was a learning period and a time for exploring ideas and developing leaders. The key leader was Judge Reuben P. Boise of Salem, Oregon, who served as the fourth Oregon State Grange master 1880 to 1887 and then served as the sixth master in 1892-1894.

More successful was the attempt to establish a fire insurance program. Studies began in 1875 based on California experience. Bylaws were adopted in 1884, and in 1886 the Lower Columbia River Fire Relief Association was in operation and providing substantial savings. An early leader was F.C. Yeomans of Washougal, Clark County. Later the name was changed to Grange Mutual Insurance Company and the firm still operates in Oregon.

The Oregon State Grange took a keen interest in organizing Granges in Washington Territory. At the 1873 organizing session the Oregon delegates elected five of the new Oregon State Grange officers from the Walla Walla area. Oregon's farms were concentrated at that time in the Willamette Valley, as were the Oregon Granges. Walla Walla was thus 250 miles away, but the Grangers from Walla Walla attended the Salem, Oregon, sessions until 1884. Thereafter, the Washington Territory representation came mostly from Skamania, Clark and Lewis counties.

In 1874, the Oregon master personally organized Granges in Washington Territory. Several dedicated Washington deputies brought the roster of Granges in Washington Territory to 63 by the end of 1874. Three were added in 1875 and two in 1876, then none until two more in each of 1883 and 1884, and then none until 1889. Factors of transportation and communications plus Oregon's internal problems left the new Washington Granges pretty much on their own. Most died in infancy. By early 1889, there were only six Granges left in Washington Territory.

On the day it was organized, the Oregon State Grange adopted a resolution calling for improved navigation on the Willamette and Columbia rivers. The Corps of Engineers built the Cascade Canal and Lock from 1878 to 1896 at a cost of $3.8 million, bypassing the treacherous Cascade Rapids in the Columbia River Gorge.

Dredging began in 1867 to cut through the Willamette River's Swan Island bar in Portland. Ultimately, many dredging projects followed to achieve a 40-foot channel from Portland to the ocean, and with 48 feet at the Columbia River entrance.

The Army in 1885 began building the South Jetty at the mouth of the Columbia. The North Jetty was completed in 1917.

Congress authorized construction of The Dalles-Celilo Canal in 1903. It was completed in 1915.

In 1879, the Oregon Legislature was urged by Grangers to create a canal commission to regulate the Willamette Falls Locks at Oregon City. It was an early precedent, duly tested in the courts, for public regulation of utilities in Oregon. Later the Army acquired the old Willamette Falls Locks, built in 1870-1872, and rehabilitated the locks in 1915.

In 1927, Congress authorized the Corps of Engineers to prepare a comprehensive plan for utilization of the Columbia River and tributaries for power, navigation and other purposes. The 1932 report led to the start of construction of Bonneville Dam in 1933 and Grand Coulee Dam in 1934. Many other projects followed. Bonneville Dam flooded the Cascade Rapids and resulted in the retirement of the Cascade Canal and Lock.

The Willamette River portion of the Columbia River and tributaries program included about half of the Army dams, numerically. These were generally for flood control and power, and resulted in increasing the effective agricultural acreage of the fertile Willamette Valley. Power from Willamette River dams was particularly valued because high stream flows came in winter when power was most needed to carry peak loads, and the proximity to population centers required little transmission.

Throughout the massive Columbia River and tributaries development program the Grangers of Oregon and Washington were heard many, many times.

CHAPTER FIVE

1889 - 1905

FARMERS ORGANIZE ON THE WASHINGTON FRONTIER

"Go West, young man, go forth into the country."
Horace Greeley, 1837

"Up to our own day, American history has been in a large degree the history of the colonization of the Great West. The existence of an area of free land, its continuous recession, and the advance of American settlement westward, explain American development."
Frederick Jackson Turner, 1893

Washington is a young state, and is in many ways still an evolving frontier. The 1989 Centennial emphasizes its robust youth. A century hence, it will still be a young state relative to almost all other states.

The year 1989 marks another Centennial. Washington farmers, in 1889, organized the Washington State Grange, just two months before statehood. The 16 years from 1889 to 1905 cover the pioneering period of the Washington State Grange as it struggled for survival.

When Washington became a state in 1889, the occasion was used to announce the closing of the American frontier. This came only 52 years after Greeley in 1837 advised young people to cross the Appalachians. The Director of the Census in 1890 declared that the boundary between inhabited areas and uninhabited areas of free land had disappeared. The frontier was gone. This led historian Frederick Jackson Turner (1861-1932) to deliver his famous 1893 paper, "The Significance of the Frontier in American History." It became a classic in American historical writing In symbolizing the passing of the frontier, the state of Washington was not alone. Montana, South Dakota and North Dakota also became states in 1889, and in 1890 Congress admitted Idaho and Wyoming.

The Role of the Railroads. Statehood did not come in a covered wagon via the Oregon Trail as in the case of Oregon in 1859. For the northern tier states of 1889 and 1890 statehood came by rail with a million people. Including Oregon, these seven states from 1880 to 1890, gained over 1,030,000 people, increasing from 478,000 to 1,509,000. North Dakota, with the earliest service by several railroads, enjoyed a fivefold jump from 37,000 to 191,000 people followed by Washington's 75,000 to 357,000 people, surpassing Oregon's 318,000 total.

The railroads opened the country and brought the people. But the northern railroad routes almost were not authorized. In 1853, when Isaac Stevens started west to make a railroad survey and become the first governor of Washington Territory, the secretary of war was Jefferson Davis. Davis, later the president of the Confederacy, favored the idea of a transcontinental railroad as close to the Mexican border as possible. He favored only a southern route and the extension of slavery. His views had strong Southern support in Congress.

When the Southern states seceded in 1861, and vacated their seats in Congress, the stage was set for moving ahead on legislation which the Southern reactionaries had opposed. In rapid order in 1862, President Abraham Lincoln signed the Homestead Act, Morrill Act, the act creating the Department of Agriculture and the Pacific Railway Act. In 1864, he approved the Northern Pacific Railway Act authorizing the route to Puget Sound via the Columbia River Gorge. That line was built by 1883 to Portland, thence by barge to Kalama and by rail from Kalama to Tacoma. The route provided for a branch from Pasco via the Stampede Pass tunnel completed in 1887 through to both Tacoma and Seattle. Other lines followed. The Great Northern Railway was completed in 1893.

The Washington State Grange was organized in a lodge hall occupying the second floor of McMaster's store, Camas, on Sept. 10, 1889.

The land grant to the Northern Pacific was greater than the area of Washington, and the N.P. vigorously promoted the sale of its land to prospective farmers. In 1900, tree-farmer Frederick Weyerhaeuser paid $5.4 million for 900,000 acres of Northern Pacific timberland. The N. P. also had a tough policy on foreclosing on mortgages, dominating the politics of Washington Territory and arousing the ire of farmers by means of high freight rates, discriminatory practices and poor service.

The railroad issue dominated both of Washington's constitutional conventions. The calling of the first convention was triggered by an attempt of Walla Walla and Columbia counties in 1876 to be annexed to Oregon. That spurred the Washington Territorial Legislature to seek statehood by calling the first constitutional convention at Walla Walla June 11 to July 27, 1878. The proposed constitution was approved by the voters. It provided strict regulation of railroads. Congress hesitated to approve statehood. Perhaps one factor was the uncertain progress of construction of the Northern Pacific Railroad, including prolonged delays incident to bankruptcies of 1873 and 1883.

Congress approved statehood on February 22, 1889, with conditions. It required calling a new constitutional convention, voter approval of the constitution, and a review of the proposed constitution by the president as a condition of issuing the statehood proclamation. The Washington voters on May 14 elected 75 delegates to write the constitution, and the delegates met in Olympia July 4, 1889.

Some of the proposals were ominous, such as providing a friendly climate to encourage construction of railroads. The farmers, however, had no spokesman or organization. The flurry of Grange interest had fallen victim to neglect. As noted earlier, only six Granges remained active in Washington Territory. Three Washington Grangers decided to prepare for the challenge ahead.

Washington State Grange Created. At the Oregon State Grange annual session at Salem May 28-31, 1889, Caleb J. Moore, F.C. Yeomans, both of Washougal No. 69, and H.M. Knapp asked for help. The response appears in the Oregon 1889 proceedings as an adopted resolution: "Having considered the welfare of Washington Territory, we believe that it would redound to the good of the whole to aid that Territory in the rebuilding of the Order within its borders. With an organized force of fifteen or twenty subordinate Granges, that Territory could then organize a state Grange of its own and the success of the work be thus assured: therefore be it

"Resolved, That Oregon State Grange authorize the Executive Committee to place the Lecturer, or his Deputy, in the field for such time as may be necessary to organize the requisite number of Granges for a state organization."

Fifteen Granges would be required to form a state Grange. On June 15 Master James Nevins of Cape Horn No. 70 organized Mount Pleasant No. 73 in Skamania County as the first new 1889 Grange. Jesse O. Wing was elected master. In July, Oregon State Grange Lecturer John Simpson organized La Camas No. 74 with H.M. Knapp as master; then added Wide West No. 75; Bear Prairie No. 76; and Preston No. 77. New Granges formed in August were Charter Oak No. 78; Mt. Valley No. 79 at Amboy; Fruit Valley No. 80; and Washington No. 82. Another Oregon Deputy S.B. Phillips formed Centerville No. 81; No. 6, No. 83 (an unusual name); Burgen No. 84; and Enterprise No. 95.

Delegates from 16 Washington Territory Granges met in the Odd Fellows' Hall in LaCamas, now Camas, on September 10-12, 1889, to create the Washington State Grange. They were:

Mt. Pleasant	Washington
Cape Horn	No.Six
Fruit Valley	La Centre
Maple Grove	Preston
Wide West	Washougal
Brush Prairie	Bear Prairie
LaCamas	Mt. Valley
Union Ridge	Charter Oak

Master H. E. Hayes, of the Oregon State Grange, was the temporary chairman. He appointed the working committees to draft bylaws, resolutions and handle other business, and then conducted the election of the first slate of officers:

Master, D.L. Russell
Overseer, J.O. Wing
Lecturer, James Nevins
Steward, S.D. Durgan
Assistant Steward, R.J. Fletcher
Lady Assistant Steward, Lizzie E. Rima
Chaplain, J.C. Allen
Treasurer, William Smiley
Secretary, A. Buchanan
Gate Keeper, J.C. Ward
Ceres, Viola Turk
Pomona, Elizabeth Russell
Flora, Alice Hutchinson
Executive committee, H.M. Knapp and Charles Zeek

Resolutions were passed thanking the Oregon State Grange for yeomanly help in forming Granges and on organizing the Washington State Grange. Two Grangers from California also received thanks. This feeling of gratitude and sense of fraternity among West Coast Grangers has become a tradition, which has since resulted in a century of continuing cooperation. Two months later when Oregon Master Hayes attended the National Grange and announced the formation of the Washington State Grange, he graciously added, "I shall not be surprised to see Washington take the lead in Grange prosperity on the Pacific Coast within a few years."

Early Grange Concerns. The main resolution and reason for the rush to get organized in September 1889 concerned the dissatisfaction with the proposed constitution of the proposed state of Washington. The constitutional convention had completed its work August 23 and the people would vote on October 1. An affirmative vote was a foregone conclusion because the issue was statehood and the constitution was incidental. Nonetheless, the Grangers decided to go on the record. They didn't go so far as to say that the Northern Pacific Railroad representatives had written the document, although some Grangers felt that way because the second constitution was weak on regulating the railroads compared to the first constitution. Here is what the Washington State Grange did say about the proposed 1889 constitution:

"First. It provides for more offices than the public service requires, and it also makes provision for the creation of offices by the courts and legislature that are uncalled for and unnecessary.

"Second. The salaries are fixed too high, with no provision for a reduction of the same, but in nearly every case it provides for an increase.

"Third. This being the case, the result will be an office-seeking class, the most worthless class that can exist. It will also foster machine politics of the most corrupt and offensive character.

"Fourth. It is calculated to encourage extravagance in the expenses of the Legislative Assembly, and also in all its appropriations, and thus to grievously overburden an overtaxed people.

"Fifth. It provides for secret sessions of the Legislature, to which we are strongly opposed.

"Sixth. It invites foreign capital to come here and obtain possession of our land, and to buy up our industries, and operate the same, and thus in time reducing our fair young state to the same conditions that Ireland occupies today. We believe that our land, our industries and our mines should be held sacred to American capital and

American industry.

"Seventh. It provides that it shall take a two-thirds vote of both houses of the Legislature to submit an amendment to the constitution to a vote of the people, thus practically prohibiting any amendment thereto.

"Eighth. For these and many other reasons we call upon the farmers, laboring men and all taxpayers to unite with us in voting down an instrument fraught with so much peril to the public welfare."

Added insight on concerns of farmers in 1889 is provided by a resolution in the form of a questionnaire to be sent to candidates for the Legislature:

"Be it resolved, by the State Grange of Washington, That it shall be the duty of the Legislative Committee of this Grange to submit the following questions to each candidate for the House of Representatives or Senate of the State of Washington and request a written answer to the same:

"Are you in favor of a Railroad Commission?

"Are you in favor of a law to fix fares and freights the same or less than those fixed in the State of Oregon?

"And will you forbid discrimination in freights and fares?

"Are you in favor of giving the Commission power to enforce the law?

"Are you in favor of taxing R.R. property as all other property is being taxed?

"What is your opinion in relation to State lands, and also school lands, and upon what terms should they be sold, and in what quantities to each purchaser; or are you opposed to the sale (of public lands) at the present time?

"Are you in favor of a mortgage tax law?

"Are you in favor of a usury law? Are you a prohibitionist or a high license?

"Are you a woman suffragist?

"Are you in favor of exempting bonds of any character, or any other property from taxation?

"Will you favor strict economy in all public matters?

"In any legislation in which the interest of the farmers and some other interest comes into conflict, which interest would you favor?

"What is your business calling?

"Who would you favor for United States Senator?

"And the Committee shall have the answers printed and distribute them among Masters of Subordinate Granges throughout this jurisdiction."

Frontier Grievances. When Isaac I. Stevens (1818-1862) became the first territorial governor of Washington in 1853, he found that his constituency was unhappy with the Hudson's Bay Company. In his first message February 28, 1854, he told the Territorial Legislature that the HBC was "usurping a large proportion of the trade, and annually carrying off great amounts of specie from the country." He urged Congress to extinguish the HBC title, and that was finally done in 1870.

During Washington's 36-year territorial period, 1853-1889, the messages of the governors ranged between two extremes. First they complained about the discouraging struggle against the indifference of Congress and federal officials. On the other hand the governors reported that "the exuberant mood of expansionism is uppermost, with its extravagant claims to rich resources and its bold expectations of future development, all too often clothed in florid eloquence."

Historian Gilbert C. Fite saw the agricultural frontiers as alternating between "Daydreams and Nightmares." The periods of boom and bust resulted in ruined, broken individuals. There was a huge gulf between imagining a Garden of Eden and achievement. He concluded "the frontier more often did the conquering."

David L. Russell (1835-1913), the first master of the Washington State Grange, served six years from September 10, 1889, to June 6, 1895.

He was born in West Virginia June 20, 1835, moved to Missouri at six, then by ox team to the gold rush at Placerville, California, in 1849. He returned to Missouri 1852, married Nancy B. Bybee, was captain of a Missouri militia company two years during the Civil War, moved to San Francisco, via New York and Panama, with a wife and two children in 1864. He took a homestead near Battle Ground in Clark County, W.T., in 1866. Nancy died at 35 of appendicitis in 1873 leaving him with the three daughters and a son, all of whom survived him. In 1875, he married Elizabeth Durgan, who had three children previously. In 1882, he bought a dairy farm on the Columbia River near Washougal. He lived in Vancouver for several years and served on the city council. Russell served in the Territorial Legislature 1873-75 and for many years as justice of the peace at Washougal. He was a Methodist, Democrat and member of Odd Fellows (I.O.O.F.) He died August 22, 1913, at 78. The 1924 State Grange session memorialized the passing of Elizabeth Russell.

Russell's Grange career included helping to organize Maple Grove No. 45 in July 1874, and serving as its first master. In 1883, he became the first master of Washougal No. 69. In 1885, he attended as a Clark County delegate at Oregon State Grange, and his wife, Elizabeth, was elected Flora serving to 1888, the only officer from Washington Territory. In 1886, he was a delegate from Columbia Council. After his six years as state master, Russell was on the state executive committee 1895-99 and 1905-07. Elizabeth served as state Pomona 1889-91, chaplain 1899-03 and 1905-07.

Russell began building Granges, and personally organized five. Washington State Grange closed 1889 with 15 Granges and 353 members. Three years of slow, steady progress reached a peak of 36 Granges and 1,219 members in 1892. The financial panic of 1893 delivered a staggering blow, followed by five years of hard times. At the end of 1894, Russell's last full year, membership was down to 868 in 28 Granges.

One bright spot in 1894 was the formation of the Washington Fire Relief Association with Russell as first president. Oregon Grangers had proposed an insurance program in 1875 and, based on California experience, got into business in 1884 as the Lower Columbia

David L. Russell

River Fire Relief Association. It had served both states until 1894. The Washington Fire Relief Association in time changed its name to Grange Insurance Association (GIA).

In the early years the Master's Address consisted of only about five printed pages. Russell's 1890 Master's Address urged Grangers "to consult together, play together, and work together." He questioned that overproduction could be the great trouble (causing low prices) when many are in hunger.

At the 1891 session in Goldendale a Granger complained, "...our homes are mortgaged—paying to money kings of the East. We work hard, live economically, deny ourselves and families all luxuries, yet we sink deeper into debt." That year the resolutions called for an inheritance tax, direct election of senators, expressed concern over foreign land ownership and favored woman suffrage. Also in 1891 there were three Grange stores operating in Clark and Skamania counties. In 1892, rural free delivery and a pure food law were demanded. At White Salmon in 1893 Grangers were miffed because the president of the board of regents of the State Agricultural College refused to allow President John W. Heston to address the State Grange. In 1894, however, a resolution commended Washington State Agricultural College for Professor Bryan's talk.

Since the Grange had no bulletin, it designated *Pacific Rural Press* of California as its house organ in 1890, and in 1892 shifted to *Pacific Northwest Farmer* as well as local papers.

The state master had no office, no employees, and he needed to be a good farmer to be able to afford being master. In 1893, the master was paid $100. This would be reduced in 1897 to $50 per year. Member annual dues were $1.50 for men, 75 cents for women.

At the Washougal session in June 1895 Augustus High was elected as the second state master.

Augustus High (1844-1927) served as state master six years from 1895 to 1901. He was born in New Columbia, Pennsylvania, on September 7, 1844, attended common schools there, headed west in 1862 settling in Yankton, capital of Dakota Territory where he fought briefly in the Indian wars of 1862. He did public surveys and in 1882 became an assistant passenger agent for the Chicago, Milwaukee and St. Paul Railway for the area west of Chicago. Secretary of the Interior Carl Schurz appointed him a special agent of the U.S. General Land Office. He married Ida V. Richardson of Philadelphia in 1877 but they had no children. He moved to Vancouver, Washington, July 1894, purchased 10 acres and went into the growing of prunes and English walnuts. While state master, he was elected to the State

Augustus High

Senate to represent Clark and Skamania counties. He had been a member of Fruit Valley Grange No. 80 and then Washington No. 82. He was initially secretary and then president of the Washington Fire Relief Association, served on the State Grange executive committee 1901-03 and 1904-05, and had organized two Granges. Ida High was State Flora 1897-99. Augustus High died September 22, 1927, at the age of 83. The State Grange in 1920 memorialized the passing of Ida.

The slide in Grange membership continued under High, bottoming at 20 Granges with 459 members the end of 1898. That year saw the average Grange size fall to a low of 23 members. Three years later, at the close of 1901, the State Grange could report some recovery to 25 Granges and 845 members. The Grange was to survive and flourish.

Although Oregon Granges are clustered mainly in the Willamette Valley, the geography of Washington Granges has been less concentrated. National Grange Deputy Garretson in 1873 visited Walla Walla which made for representation in the Oregon Grange from Walla Walla and not from lower Columbia River counties. By 1884, however, the focus shifted as Clark and Skamania counties became active.

In 1889, the geography was thrown off again because the quick, convenient way for the Oregon Grange officers to help form the State Grange in Washington was in these two counties. It led to the election of three state masters from Clark and Skamania in the 1889-1905 period. This unbalance could be explained at the time because of the great distances involved, and because of the later settlement of eastern Washington for many reasons: the Indian wars, late recognition of the Palouse capabilities and waiting for the railroads.

In his 1899 Master's Address, High noted the 35 percent increase in membership mainly in Whitman County because of the efforts of C.B. Kegley and Nicholas Ennis. The startup of the State Agricultural College at Pullman helped make Whitman a marked county. Master High also called for organization of Pomona Granges.

Augustus High kept alive the old Grange agenda and added a few items. The old resolutions were reaffirmed for postal savings banks, rural free delivery, pure food law and direct election of senators. A

Jesse O. Wing

The 1910 State Grange convention was held at Tucker in Cowlitz County. The delegates assembled for a group photograph on the steps of their convention headquarters, the Pleasant Hill Grange hall.

new resolution advocated the Nicaraguan canal. For the most part it was his unfortunate lot to deplore the poor crops, low prices, high taxes and high interest rates. The times were hard, but at least the Washington Fire Relief Association was successful, even if they sometimes had to ask members to wait on loss settlements.

One of the 1900 session resolutions from the agricultural committee urged more emphasis on livestock as a step toward a more diversified agriculture.

At the 1901 State Grange session Jesse O. Wing was elected the third state master. High and C.J. Moore were selected for the executive committee, and both High and Russell continued as directors of the fire relief association.

Jesse O. Wing (1858-1915) served as the third state master for four years, 1901 to 1905. In this brief time, the membership tripled from 845 to 2,813 and number of Granges increased from 25 to 54. Wing made effective use of deputies, particularly Kegley and Marble.

While no detailed biography is available, he is known to have been

from Syracuse, New York. He homesteaded at Mt. Pleasant in Skamania County, W.T., in 1885, and as noted was first master of the Mt. Pleasant Grange No. 73 in 1889. He raised potatoes, onions and green crops. He died in Clark County's first fatal automobile accident on November 20, 1915, at the age of 57. He had managed the Clark County Fair, and was a member of the Washougal City Council. He had long been secretary of the Washington Fire Relief Association and member of Odd Fellows. Wing had four children of his own by his first wife; his second wife had two children previously and they also adopted a girl.

Wing had served as state overseer 1889-93, master 1901-05, and executive committeeman 1906-15.

The decision to hold the 15th session of the Washington State Grange in Pullman was a master stroke. President E.A. Bryan of the State College of Agriculture welcomed the Grange. The session helped to cement good relationships and set the pattern for future sessions in Pullman. More important, the Grange had broken out of the 14-year tradition of meeting only in four southwestern counties,

Clark nine times, Klickitat three, Cowlitz and Skamania once each. Finally, the Pullman session kindled a good fire of interest in the Grange in eastern Washington.

Wing's first Master's Address quoted National Master Jones, "Educational feature of the Grange is its most important work." Wing called for educating children toward agriculture instead of away from it. The next two years he shifted to emphasis on nature study. His top legislative item was direct legislation by initiative and referendum. He was strong for good roads, saying bad roads are a much greater tax than the cost of good roads. He advocated advertising. He cited the Ewartsville Grange No. 114 near Pullman for its annual picnic and stock show. He also cited Washington No. 82 for conducting the Clark County Fair. A helping hand for creating the Idaho State Grange was urged. His last Master's Address deplored the excessive profits of International Harvester. A goal of organizing a Grange in every agricultural district was set. Finally, he again quoted National Master Jones on the meaning of education for good citizenship:

"This organization is one of the great educational forces that teaches among other things that honesty, fair dealing, giving value received in all exchanges; industry, frugality, thrift, and observing the Golden Rule are essential characteristics of good citizenship—setting its seal of condemnation on all forms of fraudulent practices, extortion or robbery, whether done under forms of law, by combination, monopoly or trust methods, or by the more vulgar practice of stealing—striving to build up a public sentiment that will ostracize the man or corporation who amasses millions of dollars in any other way than by honorable methods based on the principle of giving value received for all labor or article of value."

CHAPTER SIX

Kegley: 1905 - 1917

BY THEIR DEEDS AND BY THEIR WORDS

"Let each man think himself an act of God.
His mind a thought, his life a breath of God.
And let each try, by Great Thoughts and Good Deeds,
To show the most of Heaven he hath in him."
Phillip James Bailey

The State Grange first noticed Kegley by his deeds. Soon he would become known for his words as well, in Whitman County and statewide and at National Grange sessions. He was a leader.

As early as 1899, Master Augustus High observed the 35 percent rise in Grange membership due largely to the efforts of Kegley and Nicholas Ennis in Whitman County. Master Jesse Wing made vigorous use of his deputies for organizing new Granges and especially praised Kegley and D.L. Marble. Kegley more than passed his apprenticeship.

The 1905 election of Kegley as the fourth state master built a fire for the State Grange in eastern Washington and soon statewide in both membership and legislative achievements.

Kegley set a high standard of leadership, energetic drive and perseverance. At the local level his deputies organized Granges. At the state level the Grange won a major victory in 1912 in the initiative and referendum, as well as other legislative gains. At the national level Kegley helped win some legislation and worked hard at selling Western progressive ideas to the National Grange.

Carey B. Kegley (1857-1917) served as the fourth Washington State Grange master for 12 years from 1905 to 1917, when he died in office.

He was born in Ohio on March 25, 1855, and soon moved to Ames, Iowa. No biography is available, but it is intimated that he studied under Professor P.H. Holden at Iowa Agricultural College in Ames. He moved to Washington in 1891 and for two years was engaged in merchandising at Palouse, Washington. He began growing wheat. He became a charter member of old Pine Grove Grange in March 1899, and in May he organized Whelan No. 117. He organized eight Granges before and 18 after becoming state master in 1905, for a total

Carey B. Kegley

of 26 Granges. He organized Palouse No. 177 in 1906 and became a member. While doing land appraising for the Federal Land Bank, Kegley died of pneumonia and pleurisy on October 29, 1917. His wife Augusta M. Kegley was state Ceres 1913-23. When she died at 82 in November 1940 she had 65 years of Grange service, starting at age 17 in Iowa.

Blessed Are They Who Organize Granges. From 1905 to 1917 the U.S. farm economy was more up than down. The 1907-1908 financial panic and the mild recessions of 1911 and 1914 dampened a generally healthy, growing economy. Kegley took the ups and downs in stride to expand Grange membership fivefold.He called for a Pomona Grange in every county.

Washington State Grange membership experienced its longest continuous annual growth in the 14 years from 1898 to 1912. Only 20 Granges remained in 1898 with a low of 459 members. In the next seven years High and Wing brought this up to 54 Granges with 2,813 members. Here Kegley and his deputies took over. In seven years, 1905-1912, they added 281 Granges by years as follows: 15, 21, 29, 65,

76, 42, and 33. Year after year Kegley could report that Washington led the nation in organizing new Granges for the year. Membership increased sixfold from 2,813 members to 17,029. The next three years, however, experienced a net loss of 25 Granges, falling from 335 to 310 and a loss of 4,023 members, or more than 20 percent, to 13,006. In his last two years Kegley added 29 Granges and brought the membership to 14,336 by the end of 1917. An added benefit was the growth in the average number of members per Grange from 23 to 42. Kegley was proud of the increase in Pomona Granges from five to 25.

The key to Kegley's success was the deputy system. From his own experience in Whitman County 1899 to 1905 in organizing eight Granges, and then 18 more after he became state master, Kegley looked upon the work of every deputy in organizing a Grange not as a cost but as an investment in the future of the Granges. Moreover, the training of deputies was likewise an investment in the future because many deputies had served their apprenticeship under Kegley just as he had served under High and Wing. Many deputies later stepped into higher positions of leadership.

Among the at-large and special deputies were William Bouck who organized 35 Granges, 15 under Kegley; Charles E. Cline, 18; Fred J. Chamberlain, 22, with 15 under Kegley; C.E. Flint, 59, with 58 of them in the Kegley period; C.W. Frase, 17; W.H. Kaufman, 21; Fred W. Lewis, 30; Fred Nelsen, 15, with five under Kegley; H.L. Noble, 46; Sam T. Shell, 29; Ernest M. Smith, 38; Alson W. Steers, 10; Frank P. Waters, 92 of which 18 were under Kegley; and Jesse Wing, nine with six under Kegley. Many other deputies served only local areas: D.J. Davis, 11 in Clallam and Kitsap counties; C.N. Hogan, 10 in Cowlitz County; S.G. Schoonover of Clark County, 12, with 11 in Kegley's time; and H.E. Wells, 10 in Skagit County. Dozens of other deputies each formed one to nine Granges.

This may read like the biblical "begats" and indeed begetting is the work of the deputy. Kegley could well have added that the Beatitudes might have included a special blessing for those who organized Granges.

Coalitions For The Public Interest. Grangers at the 18th annual session of the Washington State Grange in 1906 in Spokane heard a new voice—clear, energetic, courageous and persuasive. The Master's Address set a theme and pattern that would soon become familiar. Kegley faulted the National Grange for rejecting a resolution endorsing direct legislation. He attributed this unprogressive attitude to three failings, which he had observed at his first National Grange session of November 1905 in Atlantic City. First, the national body was not representative in its voting. Second, it did not properly account for its expenditures. Third, it did not promote formation of new Granges. In his opinion, reforms were needed, and the Washington State Grange delegates agreed. It remained to be seen whether Kegley was courageous or foolhardy.

One lesson Kegley learned on his first trip east was the importance of finding allies and promptly organizing with them. The issue involved repealing the federal excise tax on denatured alcohol. He found support among the other progressive Grangers and also among manufacturers who used denatured alcohol. He proposed and the delegates approved the idea of working with others. As a result of this lesson, Kegley in 1910 took the lead with six other state Granges in forming the Conference of Progressive Granges. Each year the Conference met in connection with the National Grange. After hearing talk about parcel post service for 20 years, the Grange progressives began getting results in two years and then went on to fight for the postal savings system. In 1913, the Conference of Progressive Granges began working with other farm groups and formed the Farmers' National Council and set up an office in Washington, D.C., with George P. Hampton in charge. The venerable Oliver Hudson Kelley, founder of the National Grange, was one of the progressives and often met with them until he died in 1913. Kegley knew him well.

More importantly at the state level, Kegley recommended in his 1906 Master's Address that a special committee be appointed to "earnestly cooperate with the State Federation of Labor's committee on legislation." The committee was formed and also was instructed to attend the legislative session at Olympia.

The decision for country and city areas to collaborate may have been a factor in the enactment of the direct primary law of 1907 and its incidental provision that, in effect, amounted to direct election of U.S. senators starting in 1908. The 17th amendment requiring voter election of U.S. senators was adopted in 1913.

By 1908, the collaboration had resulted in Grange support for a workman's compensation law and an eight-hour day for working women. This year marked a clear-cut decision of Grangers to support a public interest issue that was not inherently a farm issue or concern. Incidentally, C.R. Case, the representative for the State Federation of Labor, was a Granger and addressed the State Grange sessions.

Informal collaboration at Olympia helped to achieve the constitutional amendment for women's suffrage in 1909, and voted by the people in 1910, and passage of constitutional amendments for the initiative, referendum and recall, to be voted on by the people in 1912. To prepare for the 1912 election, a meeting was held in Yakima September 26, 1911, to form the Joint Legislative Committee consisting of the Direct Legislation League of Washington, Washington State Federation of Labor, Farmers' Union and the State Grange. These organizations, which were brought together by Kegley as a coalition for the public interest, carried the elections of 1912.

The Progressive Era. Kegley was fortunate in that his 12 years as master (1905-1917) came during the Progressive Era, the period from the end of the Spanish American War to the U.S. entry into World War I. In fact, Theodore Roosevelt was in his fourth year in office when Kegley became master.

The Progressive Era brought about many reforms to overcome both corruption in government and highhanded conduct by big business. Theodore Roosevelt symbolized the Progressive Era and Woodrow Wilson completed many more reforms in his first four-year term. Theodore Roosevelt identified himself with the farmer and Kegley identified with Roosevelt.

Theodore Roosevelt (1858-1919) was born in New York City. He early took an interest in nature. Starting in 1884, for two years he went into cattle ranching in North Dakota at which he lost money but gained a better understanding of farming and of the West.

As president he sponsored creation of the Reclamation Service and the Forest Service. He started construction of the Panama Canal, which soon exerted a regulatory influence on railroad freight rates. He launched the conservation movement and dramatized it by convening the First Governors' Conference at the White House. It was entirely devoted to conservation. He also created a number of conservation commissions. He preached the lessons of stewardship of the soil and all natural resources by the farmer and all Americans.

Country Life Commission Reports. Theodore Roosevelt, like Franklin Delano Roosevelt, was a friend of the farmer. On August 10, 1908, as president he established the Country Life Commission under the chairmanship of Dr. Liberty Hyde Bailey, dean of the College of Agriculture at Cornell. The report of January 1909 revealed the deplorable living conditions and the poverty level income on many American farms.

In his message of February 9, 1909, transmitting the Report of the Country Life Commission the first Roosevelt said, "It is the obvious duty of the Government to call the attention of farmers to the growing monopolization of water power. The farmers above all should have that power, on reasonable terms, for cheap transportation, for lighting their homes, and for innumerable uses in the daily tasks on the farm." The report's plea for cooperatives was the forerunner of action. It said, "The introduction of effective agricultural cooperation throughout the United States is of first importance...Organized associative effort (cooperatives) may take on special forms... It may have for its object the securing of telephone service, the extension of electric lines, the improvement of highways, and other forms of betterment." The recommendation to encourage farmer-owned cooperatives was met with "venomous hostility" by the Congress, which refused to print the report of the commission.

We Must Be Good Stewards. Theodore Roosevelt viewed the imperative necessity for conservation as a moral issue based on the Golden Rule of personal relations. He translated the Golden Rule, as applied to conservation, to call for the use of resources for the greatest good for the greatest number forever. This is the moral principle of conservation. He admonished every citizen to be a good steward, in these words: "We've got to be good stewards of the resources entrusted to us."

He explained: "The conservation of our natural resources and their proper use constitutes the fundamental problem which underlies almost every other problem of our national life. Unless we maintain an adequate material basis for our civilization, we cannot maintain the institutions in which we take so great and so just a pride; and to waste and destroy our natural resources means to undermine this material basis... Yet, hitherto as a Nation we have tended to live with an eye single to the present, and have permitted the reckless waste and destruction of much of our natural wealth.

"Conservation means development as much as it does protection. I recognize the right and duty of this generation to develop and use the natural resources of our land; but I do not recognize the right to waste them, or to rob, by wasteful use, the generations that come after us.

"I ask nothing of the nation except that it so behave as each farmer...behaves with reference to his own children. That farmer is a poor creature who skins the land and leaves it worthless to his children. The farmer is a good farmer who, having enabled the land to support himself and to provide for the education of his children, leaves it to them a little better than he found it himself. I believe the same thing of a nation. The great natural resources which are vital to the welfare of the whole people should be kept either in the hands or under the full control of the whole people... for the benefit of all our people, and not monopolized for the benefit of the few... This applies to coal, oil, timber, water power, natural gas. Either natural resources of the land should be kept in the hands of the people and their development and use allowed under leasing arrangements (or otherwise): or, where this is not possible, there should be strict governmental control over their use.

"Of all the questions which can come before this nation, short of the actual preservation of its existence in a great war, there is none which compares in importance with the great central task of leaving this land even a better land for our descendants than it is for us, and training them into a better race to inhabit the land and pass it on. Conservation is a great moral issue, for it involves the patriotic duty of insuring the safety and continuance of the nation."

The turn of the century and the advent of Theodore Roosevelt to the presidency marked the shift of the U.S. from a preponderance of rural population to urban. Farmers had constituted 90 percent of the population in the first census of 1790. They were only at 60 percent of the population by 1860. The farmer became an ever smaller percentage of the U.S. population, yet had to provide food for an ever growing population.

National Tribute At Mount Rushmore. Theodore Roosevelt was the fourth president selected by Sculptor John Borglum (1867-1941) for Mount Rushmore to symbolize the democratic ideals of the nation. If he had wanted to portray four outstanding friends of the American farmer, however, he could not have done better than to choose George Washington, Thomas Jefferson, Theodore Roosevelt and Abraham Lincoln. The four presidents believed firmly in the agricultural worth of the nation. In the nation's first 150 years, they helped make the United States safe for the farmer's way of life and to keep the door open to the ideal of the family farm. They also had much to say about agriculture.

Mount Rushmore is truly impressive. The first view of the four faces at the top of Mount Rushmore comes as a surprise. Against the somber dark gray rock of the Black Hills of South Dakota appear these almost white, cameo images.Like the silver lining of the black storm cloud, they "seem apparell'd in celestial light."

There is nothing cameo-like about the scale of the carved faces. Each is about 60 feet high. Located in an arc of rock near the top of the 6,202 foot Mount Rushmore, the four presidents gaze out to the southeast, far above and beyond the valley floor 500 feet below. If the carvings had feet, the length of the statues would be 465 feet, almost as high as the Washington Monument. They would be massive, Paul Bunyan figures dominating the mountain valley. Merely to carve the faces required the removal by dynamiting, drilling and air hammering of 450,000 tons of granite rock.

Women's Suffrage. One of the early achievements of Kegley's new political coalition was women's suffrage. The National Grange was organized in 1867 with full and equal membership for women largely because of the vision of Miss Caroline Hall. But it would take 53 more years of effort before woman suffrage would be written into the U.S. Constitution by the 19th amendment to the Constitution on August 26, 1920.

Washington Territory had women's suffrage briefly from 1883 to 1887. In the October 1, 1889, vote on the adoption of the Constitution for the State of Washington, two issues were listed separately on the ballot, prohibition and women's suffrage, and both were defeated despite support by the newly formed Grange.

Mount Rushmore memorializes four presidents who made significant contributions to American agriculture.

National Park Service photo

The Washington State Grange had been on record in favor of women's suffrage since 1889. The Constitution of Washington State was finally amended 21 years later, in 1910, to adopt women's suffrage. Kegley, however, was subsequently involved in two sharp debates at the National Grange sessions of 1914 and 1915, over the procedure for achieving women's suffrage. In 1914, while unanimously in favor of woman suffrage, the National Grange voted against a federal amendment on the grounds of states' rights. The next year Kegley, as chairman of the committee, recommended in favor of a women's sufferage amendment to the U.S. Constitution, and was able to obtain a favorable 30-to-25 vote at the November 1915 National Grange session. In his Master's Address Kegley pointed out that the 25 votes constituted a measure of the reactionaries still resisting progressive policies. The key paragraph of his report read as follows:

"On behalf of the National Grange your committee views with keen satisfaction the present encouraging position of the woman suffrage movement. We are proud of the fact that the Grange was the first great body in this nation to adopt woman suffrage, and to safeguard it by providing for the equality of women with men in the exercise of all rights, privileges and governing powers in its organic laws. Thus the Grange having, both by precept and example, been the pioneer in this 'new freedom,' it is eminently fitting it should take a foremost stand in the movement to give to all women their right of suffrage."

Initiative, Referendum and Recall. The foremost legislative achievement of the Washington State Grange prior to World War I was the enactment of the initiative, referendum and recall. The Grange was not alone in this effort but it provided the keystone for the arch. By providing the means for direct legislation by the people, it strengthened democracy in America.

Writing in 1950, Professor Joseph D. LaPalombara said, "The important factor to be noted at the outset is that...there exists almost complete unanimity in the conviction that the advent of the initiative and referendum must be regarded as one of the most important landmarks in the history of American political institutions within the twentieth century."

Direct legislation specifically means the initiative, referendum and recall, and is so used here. It is sometimes broadly used to include the Australian ballot, proportional representation, direct election of senators, women's suffrage, universal suffrage, corrupt practices laws, the voter's pamphlet, and the direct primary and blanket

When Granges were being organized in the Pacific Northwest, farm life was remote and full of hardships. The Grange gave farm families a social outlet as well as a vehicle for improving their way of life. Pictured is the S. Timmons farm in Walla Walla County.
University of Washington Library photo, Special Collections Div., Neg. No. 8310

primary.

Precedents for direct legislation have long existed in Switzerland's cantons and New England town meetings. A referendum was considered when the Oregon Constitution was written in 1857. Oregon pioneered the initiative and referendum after enduring several decades of extreme political corruption. This is illuminated in C.J. Thompson's 1929 master's thesis at the University of Oregon:

"Oregon enjoyed the unenviable reputation of having one of the most corrupt and inefficient governments to be found north of Mexico and west of Pennsylvania... As soon as the Legislature convened a troop of prostitutes quite regularly convened at Salem—the lawmakers, in some cases, attaching them to the state payroll. Drunkenness and debauchery commonly prevailed throughout the whole legislative session."

In his 1903 inaugural address Oregon Governor G.E. Chamberlain appraised the 1902 election results:

"The people have seen fit to adopt an amendment to the Constitution for the initiative and referendum. Official extravagance and a disregard for the best interests of the commonwealth by legislative bodies originated the demand for the innovation. Legislative contests over the election of United States senators, and lobbies in the interest of railway and other corporations have so obstructed legislation in years gone by, that many laws actually demanded have failed of enactment, while others absolutely without merit and vicious in their tendency have found lodgement in the statute books. As a means to check these evils—sins of omission and commission—the initiative and referendum is to be attempted and there is no question but that the effect will be beneficial."

President Theodore Roosevelt made this comment on the Oregon system: "The movement for direct popular government in Oregon...was in part the inevitable consequence of the betrayal of their trust by various representatives of Oregon in the national and state legislatures."

Because of his strong leadership in advancing the initiative and referendum, William S. U'Ren (1859-1949) has long been hailed as the father of the Oregon system. He worked with labor and farm groups, including the Oregon State Grange, throughout the 1890s to obtain legislative approval and on June 2, 1902, a 72.8 percent favorable vote of the people. Only South Dakota, in 1898, adopted the reform before Oregon. In the case of Oklahoma, the reform was written into the original Constitution, and was accepted by Congress in admitting Oklahoma to statehood in 1907. In Oregon the initiative includes authority to initiate amendments to the Constitution, something that has not been achieved in Washington.

In the state of Washington, both Wing and Kegley made the initiative and referendum their top legislative goal. Kegley's experience in Washington, D.C., in advocating the repeal of federal taxes on denatured alcohol showed the necessity of working with other groups including industrial users. It is also a lesson Kegley observed when Oregon adopted direct legislation in 1902.

It took five years to apply the lesson of legislative allies to achieve direct legislation. The first taste of success was the passage of the direct primary law in 1907.

Previously, the selection of candidates for state and federal offices was left to the two predominant political parties, and in fact to a very few leaders within each party who could control the respective party conventions. The direct primary law enabled interested candidates to file a declaration of candidacy and pay a filing fee which thereupon entitled the candidate to a place on the primary ballot for the party of the candidate's choice. The people then voted to select the top candidate for each party. The leading candidates then faced each other at the general election in November. Local government elections used much the same procedure. For nonpartisan elections the direct primary reduced the field to two names for each position and these names appeared on the general election ballot. Not the least of the effects of the 1907 direct primary law was the encouragement given to the advocates of good government.

The initiative enables people to pass laws by means of petition to place the proposed law on the ballot. An alternative is a petition to the Legislature requesting passage of the law. If not enacted by the Legislature, the proposal automatically goes to the electorate for a vote. Initiatives cannot be vetoed by the governor and when enacted may not be amended or repealed within two years.

The referendum enables the voters to approve or disapprove legislation which is "referred" to the voters. Constitutional amendments are automatically referred. The Legislature may refer a bill which it has passed and the people, by prompt notice and petition, can demand a referendum on a legislative enactment.

The assumption that direct legislation is a substitute for the Legislature is not valid. Direct legislation supplements the purpose and work of the Legislature, and legislatures often make use of the referendum procedure. The real targets of the Grange and other advocates of direct legislation are the powerful corporate interests and lobbying forces which corrupt the legislative process by unreasonable lobbying, by inordinate campaign contributions and by selecting candidates for the Legislature and state offices and financing their campaigns.

Kegley referred to the corrupting influences in his last Master's Address (1917) when he identified them as the "Fish, Sawdust and Whiskey Ring." Earlier Grange proceedings refer to the railroad corporations and the money power. The saloon trust was identified as the main opponent to women's sufferage. The Grange supported and helped put across prohibition in Washington in 1914 even before the 18th amendment was adopted nationally.

The Grange success in the initiative, referendum and recall, and the voters pamphlet proved to be a temporary victory. The seven initiative and referendum measures on the ballot in 1914 served to clarify that the secretary of state cannot intervene in initiatives and referenda aside from his strictly ministerial function of counting the number of valid signatures. Also, Grangers learned that proposed laws should be carefully selected as to meaningful subject matter and must be carefully written so as to be easily understood. Of the seven Grange-sponsored initiatives, five made it on the ballot but only one was approved by the voters. It prohibited charges by private employment agencies, and was soon found to be unconstitutional. The initiative for prohibition simultaneously sponsored by the Anti-Saloon League was approved in 1914. It was not Grange-sponsored but had Grange support. The conservative secretary of state did much damage by demanding $200 per page of the voter's pamphlet. The sponsors declined to pay saying that they were entitled to the space, and the Legislature later agreed when it amended the law.

The most effective opposition came from the Stop-Look-Listen League made up of the big corporations. They seized on the complexity issue and used the motto, "when in doubt, vote NO."

The 1915 Legislature, more than ever, was controlled by the forces of reaction, and these forces proceeded to dismantle the entire package of direct legislation. The Grange and its allies promptly invoked the referendum of seven bad bills. All seven were roundly defeated in the 1916 election by margins from two to one to four to one.

Foundation of the Modern Grange. While direct legislation is Kegley's outstanding contribution toward better government in the state of Washington, Grangers have their own special reasons to honor him for laying down the foundations of the modern Grange in this state.

He pleaded for Grange halls as a way of achieving permanence

Mechanization made a dramatic impact on Washington farms during the early years of the twentieth century. The 1911 grain crop near Almira was harvested by the crew below.
University of Washington Library photo, Special Collections Div., Neg. No. 6888

both for the individual Grange and as a major community meeting center for others. By the end of 1917 there were 107 Grange-owned halls.

He converted the talk about a Grange bulletin into action. State Lecturer A.A. Kelly issued a four-page monthly bulletin from 1905 to 1907. In 1908, the Oregon State Grange proposed a joint effort. The *Pacific Grange Bulletin* was printed as an eight-page monthly in Oregon with space shared equally. It ran four years and grew to 16 pages.

The *Agricultural Grange News* was launched October 1, 1912, with Fred W. Lewis as first editor. It went from monthly to semi-monthly, to weekly, to semi-monthly and since 1980 back to monthly. "Agricultural" was deleted from the title in 1927. The Grange News has become a treasured source of Grange history.

Two other publications were printed annually. The Roster evolved to its present role as a directory of all Washington Granges. The Proceedings, grown to an average 300 pages, now requires and has an index. The Master's Address in Kegley's time usually covered about 25 subjects many of which were perennial and also served as umbrellas for related topics. Major subjects were postal service, education, cooperation (including insurance), good roads, conservation, rural credit, tax reform and public ownership of utilities. These topics were in addition to many housekeeping items. The fire insurance program enjoyed steady growth. Many Grange stores came into being and were especially successful in King County where Grange Wholesale had a major warehouse. These ventures also resulted in growth of membership.

In the educational field the report of President Theodore Roosevelt's Country Life Commission in 1909 led Kegley to launch a campaign for rural high schools on a county basis. Relations between the Grange and the Agricultural College at Pullman continued to grow favorably.

In 1913, Kegley helped sponsor tours by Iowa State University Professor P.H. Holden, his old professor at Ames, for his alfalfa lectures. In eastern Washington Holden urged combining livestock and grain farming as part of a diversification strategy using crop rotation for better soil conservation and broadening income away from the risks of one-crop farming. Holden was sponsored by International Harvester, a company that Kegley felt was earning excessive profits on farm machinery sales.

Another source of pride with Kegley was the formation of the Idaho State Grange, in which he had a hand.

Kegley's Long Reach. The long reach of history is illustrated by Kegley's involvement in creating the National Popular Government League on December 6, 1913, with Senator Robert L. Owen as president and Judson King as secretary. The Washington State Grange affiliated with the National Popular Government League in 1914. The office was in Judson King's home in Washington, D.C. Many U.S. senators and representatives belonged.

Originally aimed at direct election of U.S. senators, the league shifted its focus to conservation of natural resources, the development of water power and advancement of rural electrification, among other issues. Since his neighbor, Senator George Norris, didn't drive an automobile, Judson King regularly did the driving to work while discussing the electric power issues.

In 1948, as executive secretary of the Northwest Public Power Association, the author became a member of the National Popular Government League and often visited the Judson King home, especially for a Sunday noon breakfast of chicken and dumplings. King's book, *The Conservation Fight*, was printed soon after he died July 4, 1958, at the age of 86. The league died with him, 45 years after Kegley helped organize it.

By Great Thoughts and Good Deeds. Veneration for Kegley had been apparent long before he died. Grangers liked his thoughts. They liked his deeds. They bowed with him in his humility. He was more than respected. In him they saw reverence; they felt reverent in his presence. He had a mystic quality. His favorite poem was Kipling's "If." Here are the first four and last four lines:

If—

"If you can keep your head when all about you
Are losing theirs and blaming it on you,
If you can trust yourself when all men doubt you
But make allowance for their doubting too;

\+ + +

"If you can fill the unforgiving minute
With sixty seconds' worth of distance run
Yours is the earth and everything that's in it
And—which is more—you'll be a man, my son!"

The tributes of Kegley continued for several years following his death. The Grange provided a gravestone. The main resolution created the Kegley Memorial Fund with the intention of financing a home for elderly Grangers. The fund, however, was not adequate for so ambitious a project so the focus has been shifted to student loans and scholarships.

The Kegley Memorial Fund is still there serving to finance the education of sons and daughters of Grangers. It is also financing the Grange's historical activities. In these ways it is a memorial to remind us that a significant man had lived and for a dozen years had led the Grange. Kegley was a man of the people, who died in their service. Of him, too, it can be said as Abraham Lincoln did at Gettysburg, that he "...shall not have died in vain—that this nation, under God, shall have a new birth of freedom—and that government of the people, by the people, for the people, shall not perish from the earth."

CHAPTER SEVEN

1917 - 1922

TO MAKE US BEAR WITH PATIENCE

"If everyone were clothed with integrity, if every heart were just, frank, kindly, the other virtues would be well-nigh useless, since their chief purpose is to make us bear with patience the injustice of our fellows."

Jean Baptiste Moliere

"If all men were angels we wouldn't need a government."

James Madison

A trial by fire awaited Washington Grangers in the five years from 1917 to 1922. It was a period in which the Washington State Grange was accused of being disloyal to the war effort and new State Grange Master William Morley Bouck was even charged with violations of the Espionage Act—all apparently because of Grange views on war profits and other progressive Grange ideas.

The annual Grange session at Walla Walla in 1918 was interrupted and broken up by a mob. The new master was harassed and eventually driven from office. Additional information on what actually happened lay buried in Department of Justice files until Professor Carlos A. Schwantes did his commendable research and published a summary in 1981. The research showed that Bouck had been set up as a scapegoat and that the Grange, far from being unpatriotic, was victimized by business interests who swept vital public issues under the rug of patriotism.

Schwantes published his summary of the investigation in three articles in 1981 and 1985 and these disclosed what the Justice Department knew in 1918, that the Grange and Bouck had indeed been framed by the Employers Association of Eastern Washington, an organization of businessmen. For a long time Grangers preferred not to talk about the Bouck period; the episode became a skeleton in the closet. Dr. Schwantes, however, has done more than straighten out a few "facts." He has illuminated the process of policy making procedure and balancing the strategy and tactics of developing practical legislative programs that would hold promise of making progress toward the ideal goals of the Grange. Important lessons were learned. In some respects this period marked a transition between the old and the new Grange in Washington State.

The Uneasy Period. In the uneasy period of 1916 when Wilson was reelected president because "he kept us out of the war," Grangers complained that the price of farm produce was not rising fast enough to keep up with the European war inflation. When the U.S. entered the war, Wilson's Eastern establishment view of the United States took the form of price control on farm products but virtually no restraints on what the farmer had to buy in an economy plagued by war shortages. Wilson's secretary of agriculture was a non-farmer politician. The draft stripped the rural areas of young men and increased the demand for farm machinery and increased the mortgages to pay for it. In addition, of course, the economy worsened. The year 1921 marked a sharp economic recession that became one of the longest and deepest depressions in the history of American agriculture, lasting almost two decades. The boom of the 1920s was a bust for the farmers. The 1921 recession brought on a wave of farm mortgage foreclosures—and delayed tractor sales and farm mechanization more than 10 years.

The East and the larger cities had roads, electricity, telephones, medical and dental facilities, high schools and city life. Beyond the city limits the dirt roads were thick with dust in summer and mired axle-deep in mud when it rained. The cemetery tombstones told their grim story of infant mortality and women dying in childbirth. Ignorance was only one of the many factors.

Most farmers were Abraham Lincoln Republicans but the few Republican insurgent senators were no match for the Old Guard. As a result of his multitude of social and economic disadvantages, the farmer tended to cling to the old Populist ideas that had run their course 20 years earlier.

William Morley Bouck (1868-1945) became the fifth master of the Washington State Grange in 1917, when Kegley died, and served until 1921. He was born in Independence, Iowa, on September 5, 1868, of Dutch-English parents, moved to Royalton, Minnesota, in 1879, attended normal school and in 1888 began teaching. He married Lura Adelia Snow of Otsego, Minnesota, in 1891, and moved to Washington in 1893, operated a general store and became postmaster at Silverton. He took out a homestead, lived on it by 1895, worked at timber cruising, surveying, and hard rock mining. Bouck lived in Cheney 1896-97, returned to Silverton 1897-1902, thence to Sedro Woolley where he was a successful farmer. He specialized in bulbs, growing tulips, gladioli, iris and peonies. A well educated-man, he subscribed to many liberal publications. The Boucks had five children. He died Oct. 24, 1945. His wife Lura died in 1936.

William Morley Bouck

Bouck organized 35 Granges, served as overseer in 1917 and master from 1917 through 1921. Lura was chaplain 1916-1921.

He organized the Progressive Farmers starting in 1920, becoming national president in 1927. He was nominated in 1924 for vice president of the United States on the National Farmer Labor ticket.

Bouck Emphasized Kegley Policies. Bouck inherited both Kegley's admirers and detractors. Mainly he inherited the enmity of the representatives and paid agents of the special business interests. They had not paid much attention to the Grange when it was small. Now the business lobbyists viewed with alarm that Grange membership had grown from 2,813 to 14,336 under Kegley and would grow another 50 percent in the brief Bouck period to 21,021. The Grange had become a threat to monopoly business practices.

William Bouck adhered closely to Kegley's policies, and mentioned him often in his speeches. Of his death Bouck said, "...he whom the sorrows of the farmer finally broke down, was suddenly called to lay down the farmers' burden..." At the 30th annual session at Walla Walla in 1918, George P. Hampton began his tribute,

"The leader whose great work you have assembled here to commemorate, was to me, comrade, leader and dearest friend...Mr. Kegley has been...the foremost champion of progressive ideals in the National Grange... I have come across the continent to be present at this meeting...to gain new strength, new inspiration, new courage to carry forward the work he would have us do...the purpose of this great and beloved leader will be achieved if we take his word for our guide and unitedly and steadfastly work to accomplish what he pointed out so clearly must be done before the producers of the world are free." And as Mr. Hampton mentioned the "great beyond," he himself had but three years left.

Four State Grange sessions continued the tributes, Hampton in 1918 and E.E. Faville in 1919. The State Grange created the Kegley Memorial Committee and Kegley Memorial Fund in 1920. In 1921, the convention viewed a picture of the large gravestone provided by Grangers on the Kegley grave in Albion cemetery.

Mob Breaks Up Grange Meeting. The Walla Walla session had been scheduled for June 4-7, 1918. The beautiful Hampton tribute to Kegley came on Wednesday evening June 5. On Thursday June 6 at 10 p.m. the Walla Walla school board directed the Grange to vacate the building within a half hour. The excuse used by the School Board was that the Grange had forfeited the right to use the school by reelecting State Grange Master Bouck, who they claimed had endorsed the Nonpartisan League, which was alleged to be disloyal to the war effort. The 500 Grangers returned to their homes, and during the following week the Executive Committee completed the action on resolutions and reports and installed the officers.

The Walla Walla incident was duly recorded in the 1918 State Grange Proceedings, in the 1940 Harriet Ann Crawford history of the Grange and in the *Agricultural Grange News*. The Associated Press blacked out the story. Aside from the irresponsible charges of disloyalty to the war effort made by *Walla Walla Union Bulletin* publisher John G. Kelly, the incident was hardly reported in the newspapers.

The Grange executive committee sent a long telegram to President Woodrow Wilson. As reprinted in the Proceedings, it assured the President of the support of Washington Grangers in the war effort, and suggested that the allegations of the Walla Walla mob about disloyalty might be "indicative of the growing boldness of the reactionary controlled officials in large numbers of our Northwestern cities and counties and several of our states taking advantages of the war to destroy their political opponents under the pretense of disloyalty and pro-Germanism. This constant persecution of the organized farmers of the Northwest, by state and local authorities, and self-constituted patriotic societies and corrupt newspapers, on the pretense that the farmers are disloyal, has produced a situation terrible in its possible consequences." President Wilson replied that he would look into the Walla Walla episode. The resulting U.S. Department of Justice reports were finally located and studied by Pacific Northwest historian, Dr. Carlos A. Schwantes, formerly of Walla Walla and most recently of the University of Idaho.

In the National Archives, Schwantes reviewed the U.S. Department of Justice reports and correspondence regarding the attacks on the State Grange and on Bouck. The Justice Department records show that several months prior to the Grange session, the Employers' Association of Eastern Washington anticipated that the Grange might promote the Nonpartisan League. The Employers' group sent a representative to Walla Walla in late April 1918 to stir up local businessmen on the alleged danger that the Nonpartisan League would establish cooperative enterprises to compete with local businessmen. They presented a picture that was especially frightening to Walla Walla businessmen who depended on farmer purchases. Kelly's newspaper served as spokesman.

Bouck apparently received some information on the Department of Justice findings because he refers to it in his 1919 Master's Address. "Nowhere was the language condemning the treatment of Grange at Walla Walla as an outrage more scathing than that used by the Department of Justice which reviewed the case," he wrote. The information may have been relayed by Hampton.

The Nonpartisan League was organized in 1915 in Bismarck, N.D., by farmers who complained of monopolies and exploitation by grain speculators, bankers and politicians. Like the vast majority of Americans, the league at first opposed U.S. entry into World War I. The league obtained control of the state Republican Party and in 1919 succeeded in establishing a state-owned bank, grain mill and elevator, and hail, fire and tornado insurance. Despite harassment during World War I, the league spread into 12 states, but largely because of continued harassment, the league went out of existence by 1924. It gave rise to the Farmer-Labor Party in Minnesota and several nearby states.

Harassment By Justice Department. During 1918, Bouck continued making speeches around the state, loyally supporting President Wilson. Referring to Walla Walla, he criticized the press "for condoning mob violence in the name of patriotism." He advocated government ownership of railroads and utilities and also stressed that taxes should be levied to finance the war on a "pay as you go" basis.

His Grange speech of June 12, 1918, at Bow, Washington, referred to the "rich man's war." He felt wealth and war profits should be taxed rather than financing the entire war by means of Liberty Bonds. His Bow speech was marked by heckling and noise, and on driving home he had four flat tires. On August 13, he was indicted by a grand jury at Seattle for allegedly violating the just-passed Espionage Act of May 1918. Specifically, his Bow speech was interpreted as an attempt to discourage the sale of Liberty Bonds, thus interfering with the war effort. He was arrested and released on bail. Bouck's prosecutor had used the Espionage Act to send several liberals to prison under the frenzied hysteria of the war. The Department of Justice, however, kept hearing from George Hampton that Bouck was being framed. The department increasingly warned the prosecutor to reexamine the evidence. With the war over on November 11, 1918, the prosecutor moved to dismiss the case for lack of evidence on December 20, 1918. This ended Bouck's two 1918 ordeals, but Schwantes found Bouck "more alienated and more outspokenly radical than before."

Harassed By National Grange. From 1905 on, Kegley had portrayed the Washington State Grange as progressive and the National Grange as reactionary. The two philosophies headed for a showdown in the 1917 to 1921 Bouck period when it overlapped the 1920 to 1923 period of National Master S.J. Lowell, a grape grower from New York, and a staunch conservative Republican whom President Coolidge shortly appointed to the U.S. Tariff Commission.

Bouck's Master's Address of 1919 at Port Angeles was composed, almost calm, and was even kind to the National Grange. Bouck was reelected, in part because of his optimism that the post war period would see many economic improvements. The resolutions reaffirmed support for proportional representation voting in the National Grange, and retention of the railroads in government operation. The year saw much expansion of the Grange Warehouse Company. The events of 1918, while not forgotten, were left behind.

In 1919 the National Grange established the conservative T.C. Atkeson as its first legislative representative. Dr. Thomas Clark Atkeson (1852-1935) taught agriculture at West Virginia University, served as dean of the College of Agriculture 17 years and held other state positions. For 24 years he was master of the West Virginia State Grange. In the National Grange he served as overseer 1903-11, and spent six years on the executive committee, 1916-22. In 1919 he enraged Washington State Grangers by lobbying in favor of returning the railroads to private operation. With Atkeson, the National Grange was deeply involved in politics.

Bouck was bitterly disappointed because the National Grange refused to request a two-year extension of federal railway operation. He was more than disappointed when an overture by the American Federation of Labor was rejected by the National Grange.

In May 1920, the Federal Reserve Board had raised the discount rate from 5.25 to 7 percent. The index of farm prices fell from 250 (based on 1913) as of June 1920 to 110 early in 1921. This was the most severe drop in over a century. It had the effect of making all farm debt at least twice as hard to pay off, and it led to tens of thousands of mortgage foreclosures.

There was widespread disillusionment with the peace and this was reflected in the 1920 Aberdeen session of the State Grange. There was no self-determination of small nations as the global real estate was colonialized. There were few if any open covenants, nor was there a plan to retire the war debt. The political campaign aimed at "Back to Normalcy." The railroads were returned to private ownership and operation, and freight rates skyrocketed while farm prices declined.

National Master Lowell visited the Northwest in 1920 and his address at the Aberdeen session in 1920 received negative comment in *The Grange News*. A lady Granger meeting him on the train to Aberdeen called him anti-labor, reporting he said farmers had nothing in common with labor. She also stated he was autocratic or undemocratic. At Aberdeen, however, Lowell saw that when a charge was made against Bouck, the session immediately adopted a resolution by way of a vote of confidence.

Bouck campaigned for Congress in 1920 on the Farmer-Labor ticket running a close second after the Republican candidate. He had 40 percent of the vote.

At the National Grange convention in November 1920 in Boston, Bouck was charged and forced to stand trial on grounds of "injecting partisan politics into the Grange" and seven other charges, filed by a Yakima attorney. Three charges were thrown out. He was convicted on five trumped up charges, required to apologize, receive the National Master's reprimand and then renewed his pledge to uphold the order. It was a galling experience, and added much to Bouck's bitterness.

Bouck's Master's Address at Colville in 1921 reflected that bitterness. The *Washington Farmer* reported the speech as "reckless and intemperate" and that it showed "too much heat, hate and bitterness." National Master Lowell, a staunch New York Republican, read the speech and sent Bouck an immediate reprimand but felt that that was not enough. He called his executive committee and suspended Bouck as master pending a trial in November 1921 in Portland, Oregon, and designated Overseer Fred Nelsen to take charge of the Washington State Grange. Bouck had been reelected despite the strident Master's Address, and there were many who urged him to fight it to a finish in Portland.

The fighting spirit of the Washington Grangers was reflected in the 50 percent increase in membership 1917 to 1921 from 14,336 to a new record of 21,021. Acting Master Fred Nelsen and the executive committee offered Bouck the status of supervising deputy and continuation of salary. They encouraged him to prepare his defense and offered support.

Another blow was the death in June 1921 of George Hampton, the longtime advocate of progressive farm issues.

Bouck brooded all summer and into the fall, and then decided to break with the National Grange. He called a meeting of his supporters in Seattle on October 13 and 14, 1921. The seceders called themselves the Washington State Grange, Incorporated, but a court order prohibited their use of the Grange name. Thereupon the group adopted the name Western Progressive Farmers. About one-fourth of the Washington Grangers followed Bouck. By 1926, he converted the Western Progressive Farmers into a national organization, Progressive Farmers of America. However, his leadership became erratic, and internal problems led to wholesale loss of membership. Bouck retired to his Sedro Woolley farm. He died in 1945.

Fred Nelsen (1871-1963) became the sixth master of the Washington State Grange, serving eleven months in 1921 and 1922.

Born in Denmark in April 1871, Fred Nelsen immigrated to the U.S. in 1889, settling in Renton, Washington, as a dairy farmer. In 1898, he married Dora Jorgensen. They had a son and six daughters. Dora served as state Pomona 1919-21 and died in 1938. In 1940, he married Mrs. Meta Jonientz. She died in 1962, and he died on New Year's Eve of 1963.

He was a member of the White River Grange No. 238 from 1908, becoming a gold sheaf member in 1958, and also that year received the Grange leadership award. In 1917, he served in the Legislature and for 12 years was on the Washington State Planning Council. A strong cooperator, he was president of the Grange Cooperative Wholesale for 30 years, and was a member of Group Health

Cooperative of Puget Sound. He belonged to the Danish Brotherhood. He served on the school board 15 years. In 1964, the Fred Nelsen Junior High was dedicated at Renton in his memory. For a quarter of a century he was president of the Federal Land Bank of Spokane. He was State Grange overseer from 1919 to 1921, master 1921-1922, overseer 1923-25, and State Grange treasurer from 1929 to 1953. He organized 15 Granges.

Nelsen expressed a policy of reconciliation at the 55th National Grange session in Portland, Oregon, in November 1921, and again in his 1922 Yakima Master's Address, when he said: "We are again assembled for our annual session, and, this being the thirty-fourth time we have thus met, impresses the fact that the Grange is a stable institution.

"It has never been commercialized or subsidized, but of, by and for the farmer and actuated by the highest motives, it holds a record individually and collectively of unselfish service and accomplishment, which places it in a place all its own and richly entitles it to the esteem and confidence it enjoys. May this meeting maintain the high ideals and standards of citizenship as has been established the last

Fred Nelson

thirty-four years. Let us mutually resolve to labor for the good of our order, our country and mankind, remembering our motto, in essentials, unity; in non-essentials, liberty; in all things, charity."

The Grange News. As state secretary and editor, Fred W. Lewis supported the reconciliation policy. Lewis came from Thurston County, served as secretary a record 30 years beginning in 1907, until his death in March 1937, organizing 30 Granges while serving under Kegley. As an additional duty he began in August 1909 to edit the Washington portion of *Pacific Grange Bulletin* and when Washington began publishing its own *Agricultural Grange News* on October 1, 1912, Lewis continued as managing editor.

Editor Lewis used the paper as an educational tool and as an information service. Controversies were aired so both sides could express their opinions, and Lewis generally avoided having an opinion until the Grange had taken a position.

His opinions appeared in 30 annual reports as secretary, providing a record of continuity. In his 1922 report Secretary Lewis drew a fine line "to distinguish between purely educational discussions along the lines of government and the political action necessary to put them into effect. The former is clearly within our rights and privileges but the latter is just as clearly outside and should be left to those organizations that make their sole aim, for such action within our ranks will surely lead to dissension and rupture and will weaken our efforts in purely economical lines."

He emphasized Grange cooperative ventures notably the Washington Fire Relief Association and the Associated Warehouse Company. Time and again he called attention to the rise in membership, as in King County, as a result of the availability of Grange stores and warehouses, and he urged making these services available statewide. The State Grange often put money into these cooperatives and, in return, was able to borrow from these separate business ventures when the State Grange ran deficits, as from 1921 to 1924.

Lewis adjusted his views on the role of the Grange in politics depending on the changing sentiment. During and after the Bouck break in 1921 Lewis concentrated on keeping the conservative and moderate Grangers in the fold. He contended that the advocates of political activism had all seceded. This was not exactly the view of the executive committee even when under severe pressure, as in Portland during November 1921.

Another Confrontation. When Lowell came to Portland in November 1921 he deposed Bouck with finality. Then the National

Pacific Northwest

Agricultural Grange News

ESTO PERPETUA P H OF F H C F

VOLUME I — OLYMPIA, WASHINGTON, DECEMBER 1, 1912. — NUMBER 3

THE LAST WORD ON THE BOY SCOUT QUESTION

Beforq me upon my desk, piled higher than my typewriter, is a bundle of letters, the sort with which I have been deluged since the publication of the peace commissioners' report last summer. There is considerable variety in these letters—some of them are commendatory and brimful of congratulation, some glowing with the warmth of argument and ardent protest, but all of them testifying the keen interest felt by the Grangers of the Pacific coast in the subject of peace. Just here, before I forget it, I may say with some pride that the commendatory letters are about nine in number to one of the other sort. This is very encouraging.

All the argument, all the protest, comes from those who think the Boy Scouts are a peace organization. I have yet to receive a letter from any source that does not insist that the writer favors peace above all things; and this is encouraging again, because it shows that when the delegates in the State Grange at Snohomish and again at Puyallup responded with absolute unanimity to the call of the peace commissioner for a rally upon the "most advanced ground" upon this question, they were but reflecting the unanimous sentiment of their constituency at home. Therefore I repeat what I have said before: If there are any Grangers who believe in war or who believe in the necessity for great warlike preparations, that Granger is eccentric; that Granger is sui generis; that Granger is not keeping step with his brethren and fellows in the order. The Grange, locally, state-wide and nationally, is for absolute peace.

So far as the Boy Scouts are concerned, I am willing to admit, as one of my correspondents has said boys." He fell into bad company, over and over again, as if the repetition made the argument stronger, that in America they are "just our American boys." But our American boys may easily be led astray if we do not look well to their environments. See that drunkard reeling along the village street? That was once "just one of our American he learned to sip the inebriating cup, he fell to tippling, he began to frequent the saloons, he lost his pride and his manhood and—there he is! The coffee habit is usually learned by youngsters because they are given weak coffee in the beginning, and this is gradually made stronger and stronger as they can bear the taste and the effect of it. Rank tobacco chewing in the southern states generally begins with the mildest kind of "occasional" snuff dipping. These little things in the beginning are the very things to be watched. They are "the little rift within the lute that by and by will make the music mute." Instead of being reconciled to the Boy Scout just because it is composed of "our American boys," that fact makes me all the more solicitous about them and their environment. I for one would rather they be taught the Christian virtue of peace than that they should be prepared for that horrible relic of paganism, the hatred and butchery of warfare.

The Boy Scouts were organized and brought to prominence by a military man, avowedly for military purposes. The organization was conceived in the midst of carnage and bloodshed. Its founder's title to heroism consists in the conducting of a siege that crushed a republic off the map and substituted the rule of a foreign power, a capitalized monarchy. These facts are undenied and undeniable. The marked respect shown this "hero" of a republic's death by the Boy Scouts when he visited America shows me that he is yet a power ever in the American branch; while the first vice president of the organization in this country and the chief founder of the American branch is a man who has repeatedly declared that the best way to conserve peace is to extensively prepare for war," a sentiment that is the very opposite of the declared and unanimous platform of all Granges. The president of the organization was formerly a military governor ruling a people without asking their consent. Later on he became secretary of war and now as president of this country his course has been such as to lead many thoughtful persons to believe he desires to involve our country in a needless was with our neighbor to the southward.

Not only are these military men held up to us by the Boy Scouts as the bright particular knights exemplar of their movement, but a friend has just laid upon my desk a copy of an order dated July 12, 1912, selecting and adopting the "new Remington-UMC rifle (illustration inclosed) as the authorized rifle of the organization." It states that this rifle was designed specially for the Boy Scouts, and squads of Boy Scouts have repeatedly been seen drilling with rifles. Therefore, I say, bosh upon all its pretensions as a peace organization! There is much more to be sadi on this subject, but surely this is enough.

I am proud of the stand for peace so unanimously taken by the Washington State Grange. The National Grange is on record as assuming a position fully as strong as the state organization has adopted; but the friends of peace were shocked, astounded, amazed when the national body, under reactionary leadership suspended the work of the national peace commissioner. Brother Whitehead had done and was doing a great work in this line, and he should have been sustained—at least there are those of us who are inconsiderate enough to believe that a moiety of the ample moneys spent in prosecuting Hampton would have served our cause far better if spent in a peace propaganda.

CHAS. M. ROBINSON,
Peace Commissioner.

JUDGES AND THE INVISIBLE GOVERNMENT

(From the Chicago Tribune.)

The operations of the "invisible government" upon two branches of government, the legislative and the executive, have been dramatically illustrated. The latest disclosure shows its operations upon the judicial branch.

Here are three of the documents now published from the Hearst museum of practical politics:

This was sent to Senator M. S. Quay at Washington:

"June 28, 1898.—My Dear Senator: If it is possible for you to favor Judge Henderson of Crawford county to fill the vacancy in the superior court caused by the death of Judge Wickham I will appreciate it greatly. Of course you know all about the matter. Very truly yours,

"JOHN D. ARCHBOLD."

To William A. Stone, governor of Pennsylvania, in 1900, this letter was sent:

"Sept. 5, 1900.—Hon. William A. Stone, Harrisburg, Pa.—My Dear Governor: Will you permit me to say that if it seems consistent for you to appoint Judge John Henderson of Meadville, Pa., to the vacancy on the supreme bench caused by the death of Justice Green it will be a matter of intense personal satisfaction to me? I am sure I need not occupy your time with any argument as to Judge Henderson's fitness, either as to character or legal qualifications. With high regards, I am very truly yours,

"JOHN D. ARCHBOLD."

This was sent to J. C. Sibley, member of the House of Representatives:

(Telegram.)

"Dec. 4, 1902.—Hon. J. C. Sibley, House of Representatives, Washing-

The Grange News, which had its beginning in 1912, reflected a strong pro-peace posture as World War I approached. This issue, Dec. 1, 1912, discussed military influence in the Boy Scout movement and published the "Grange Hymn of Peace."

Grange executive committee had a long evening session with the Washington State Grange executive committee. Bouck was gone and was no longer an issue. The issue was the Washington State Grange. The focus was on the charges and demands of Yakima attorney and Granger J.R. Schwartz. His six demands were: (1) A declaration of loyalty to the National Grange, (2) an avowal of purposes to keep politics out of the Grange, (3) a reduction of salaries of state officers, (4) a change in the cooperative methods of the warehouse system, (5) disassociation of the Grange and organized labor, and (6) withdrawal of support from the Farmers' National Council.

The State Grange executive committee made no concessions, saying they were elected by all the patrons of the state and were not under the control of any local faction, according to the report in *The Grange News*, January 5, 1922.

As editor and secretary, Lewis foresaw a sharp drop in Grange membership. The work of many years would be lost. He speculated in the December 5, 1921, issue of *The Grange News* that the real cause of the spreading ruin "must be outside our organization." He said, "The Grange of Washington is progressive, but it is not extremely so."

Perhaps the Elizabethan Bard would comfort him:

"Be not dismayed, these severe afflictions
Not from the ground arise.
But oftentimes celestial benedictions
Assume this dark disguise."

CHAPTER EIGHT

GOSS: 1922 - 1933

GRANGERS WRITE A LAW

*"Lives of great men all remind us
We can make our lives sublime
And, departing, leave behind us
Footprints on the sands of time."*

A Psalm of Life
Henry Wadsworth Longfellow

Albert S. Goss left footprints on the sands of time as the seventh master of the Washington State Grange, 1922-1933, as Federal Land Bank commissioner 1933-1940, and as master of the National Grange from 1941 through 1950. Each of his three main careers marked him as a man of distinction.

But it almost didn't happen. Acting Master Fred Nelsen told the 1922 annual session that he would not be a candidate. The position was wide open. Goss was one of nine nominated. Three withdrew their names. When he finally won on the third ballot, it was by a margin of only 12 votes.

Albert S. Goss (1882-1950) was born in Rochester, New York, in 1882, the same year as Franklin D. Roosevelt. The family moved to Spokane in Washington Territory in 1889, the year Washington became a state and the Washington State Grange was formed. After business college, he became a bookkeeper in 1901, learned the milling trade, operated a flour mill, and operated a country store. He went into farming, became associated with a rural telephone company and in 1914 returned to dairy farming and joined Finley Grange No. 414 in Benton County. He married Miss Minnie E. Hand on December 21, 1907; they had three children.

In 1916, as a member of the State Grange farm credit committee, he went to Washington, D.C., on behalf of farm credit legislation. When President Wilson signed the Federal Farm Loan Act of July 17, 1916, the new law was hailed as the Magna Carta of American farm finance. Goss organized the farmers in his neighborhood into a cooperative farm loan association with a view to obtaining loans from the Spokane Land Bank. He obtained a loan himself and became thoroughly familiar with the procedure. He served as president of the local association, and in 1927 became a director of

Albert S. Goss

the Spokane Land Bank.

In 1920, Goss moved to Seattle as manager of the newly organized Associated Grange Warehouse Company, renamed in 1934 Grange Cooperative Wholesale. Among the management improvements, Goss instituted a centralized accounting and auditing service for Grange stores, and he insisted on cash transactions. State Grange Secretary Fred Lewis reported growth in Grange membership where Grange stores and warehouses did a good job. The State Grange helped Associated Grange Warehouse Company with working capital for several years even while the State Grange was operating at a deficit.

Deterioration Continues. As the newly elected State Grange master, Goss did not face a happy prospect. Grange membership continued to decline for several years before reaching the turn-around. During 1922, Grange membership had fallen from 21,021 to

14, 725 with a loss of 62 Granges from 363 to 301. Losses continued heavy in 1923 with membership dropping to 12,321 members in 276 Granges. By the end of 1925, the number of Granges had bottomed at 271 and membership rose slightly to 12,879. This was the Washington State Grange's Winter at Valley Forge. The financial deficits beginning in 1921 had required virtual elimination of the deputy system.

In 1923, the farm economy showed no improvement and Grange membership had not yet reached its low point. Yet Goss opened his first Master's Address in Bremerton in 1923 with the announcement, "Now, happily, the tide has turned."

Better Resolutions. His was a new voice in the land, new in tone, style and authority. Goss was conciliatory. He went out of his way to call attention to some progressive steps being taken by the National Grange. He also made it easy for seceded Granges to be restored. His style was moderate or low key.

Among the 50 subjects of his 1923 address Goss put emphasis first and last on avoiding resolutions that "are hastily prepared and passed without careful consideration. Our organization will carry more influence if we pass fewer resolutions and take greater care that each one passed has the fullest consideration." He also urged dividing legislative issues into two groups, those highly selective issues calling for immediate action within the year, and those requiring continuing, long-term study. In conclusion he reemphasized, "be more particular about the quality of your resolutions than about the quantity..."

In his 1924 Master's Address at Vancouver he urged, "Let us avoid promiscuous condemnation of all those who differ with us, remembering that charity of thought is one of the precepts of our order."

The ring of authority in his early addresses stems from his knowledge of finance. His training and experience as a bookkeeper undoubtedly supported his insistence on financial integrity. His discussions on taxes, electric rates and farm prices resulted from his own studies and understanding. His first year ended with a strong vote of confidence as he was reelected by a vote of 274 out of 277.

Concern About Electric Power. Under both Kegley and Bouck, the Washington State Grange had gone firmly on record in favor of public development of natural resources and public ownership of electric utilities. Goss now continued to build on this record.

In his 1923 address Goss discussed natural resources. Actually it was mostly about electric power and the good example set by

Tacoma and Seattle and their municipal utilities. He felt steps should be taken toward state development of power resources. The result was Grange adoption of a resolution in favor of initiating measures at the 1924 general election calling for state development of water power and for supporting the Bone Bill to permit cities to sell electricity outside the city limits.

The 1924 Master's Address included a table showing that Ontario, Canada, residents received electricity at less than half the rates charged by private utilities in the state of Washington. Goss urged the Grange to outline a policy regarding water power. The Washington State Grange received two suggestions to take action on power. The Washington Super Power League urged the Grange to file an initiative that would authorize public utility districts to acquire and develop water power. A resolution endorsing the proposed initiative was adopted by the Grange in June 1924.

The Seattle Local of the Electrical Workers Union had drafted a bill to create a state hydroelectric generating, transmission and distribution system. This proposal was referred to the Grange executive committee for study.

The bright spot of the 1924 election was the resounding defeat of an anti-public power bill known as the Reed bill. Its official title was Referendum No. 3. Passed by the Legislature in 1923, it proposed a prohibitive tax on cities serving outside the city limits. But electric power reformers also lost two battles in 1924. Seattle city councilman Oliver T. Erickson, a member of the Super Power League, began in 1923 to promote an initiative to create a statewide agency patterned after Canada's Ontario Hydro. Private utilities spent $175,000 on advertising against it. The initiative failed to obtain enough signatures to get on the ballot in 1924.

A bill to enable cities to serve outside the city limits, did get on the ballot as initiative measure No. 52. It was called the Bone Bill, after Homer T. Bone, a member of the Legislature and public power advocate from Tacoma. He later became a U.S. Senator and then judge on the U.S. Circuit Court of Appeals. The Bone bill went down to defeat 217,393 to 139,492 at the November 1924 election. Both measures were too little and too late. To win would require years of education of the public and then widespread public support. Goss decided to proceed with caution. In his 1925 address Goss again emphasized the discrimination in the law whereby towns and cities of Washington had authority to issue bonds and build electric systems but rural areas did not. He called for a law permitting the creation of public utility districts. He also complained that private companies were filing claim on all good water power sites.

The speech includes an example of the Goss talent for making high finance understandable to the man in the street. This is how he explained the difference between public and private power:

"Private ownership means perpetually going into debt.

"Public ownership means getting out of debt.

"One point between public and private ownership is usually overlooked. Under private ownership the tendency is to increase the capital investment either by cash investment or by inflation to the highest point on which dividends can be paid. The public pays on a constantly increasing burden.

"Under public ownership, the operation is reversed. The investment is amortized so that the public eventually is free from paying on any investment."

Goss used a railroad example to underscore this point:

"If thirty-five years ago the government had bought the railroads at their then value, inflation of values would have been avoided and 1 percent (one-half the saving in price of government money) would have completely liquidated the debt so that today we would not be paying a toll on $20,000,000,000. Authorities agree that freight rates are pyramided approximately five times before they reach the consumer. Thus this avoidable toll means a charge of approximately $250.00 per family per year."

In the campaigns which followed, the Goss explanation was changed to a comparison with home ownership: Buying public power is like buying your home. When the mortgage is paid off and you have the deed in your hand, you are truly the owner. Buying from a private utility is like renting forever, and all you ever own is a pile of rent receipts.

The Washington State Grange membership adopted resolutions favoring public ownership of Muscle Shoals, endorsed the Ontario system of power development, urged public development of power sites and adopted the master's recommendation on public ownership and development of public power. Thus by 1925 the direction of State Grange policy on electric power became more specific.

Writing the PUD Initiative. At the State Grange's 38th annual session at Kennewick in 1926, Goss showed his personal commitment to the power fight ahead. He said, "Probably the biggest trust of all times is the power trust." He again pointed out that the private utilities were filing on the water power of the nation. He called for federal government building of large hydroelectric projects, and he again called for a PUD law so rural people would have the advantages enjoyed by people served by municipal electric systems.

The Grange resolutions supported Goss.

At the 1927 session in Auburn the Grange received a report from its Intersession Committee on Power Development. Members were W.D. Lane, C.W. Riddell, and Fred J. Chamberlain. Goss reported that a PUD bill had been drafted, but lack of funds had prevented further action. The Legislative Committee recommendation to file an initiative for a PUD bill in time for the November 1928 election was adopted.

Goss gave credit for drafting the PUD law to one Granger, W.D. Lane, and five outside experts, J.D. Ross, Lewellyn Evans, Homer T. Bone, Kenneth Harlan and James Bradford. The concept of the PUD law can be traced to Ontario Hydro, the California irrigation district

A painting depicting the struggle to pass Initiative No. 1 was commissioned by Bonneville Power Administration in commemoration of BPA's 50th anniversary. Shown, left to right, are Sen. C.C. Dill, Grange Master Albert Goss, Deputy Ira Shea and Tacoma attorney Homer T. Bone. The original painting by Roger Cooke hangs in BPA's new office building in Portland, Ore.

BPA photo

laws and the very recent California Municipal Utility District Act of 1922. Chief author of the PUD law was Bone, at that time attorney for the Port of Tacoma. He used many ideas and much language from the 1911 Port Authority Act of Washington, under which the Port of Seattle was created that same year. A fierce struggle was involved in these dual accomplishments of 1911. Interestingly, the success of the movement for public ownership of the Port of Seattle grew out of the successful experience of Seattle with operatiton of two other utilities, electricity since 1905 and water since 1890. Thus many influences affected the Washington PUD bill as drafted in 1927 and 1928.

Enacting the PUD Initiative. Goss and the Grange took six years in getting the PUD issue on the ballot. It is true the Grange in 1924 was in debt and had had a serious drop in membership. The six years of talking up the PUD idea almost doubled the membership from 12,879 in 271 Granges in 1925 to 24,122 in 389 Granges in 1931. It was a classic example of gains in membership because the Grange was proposing to do battle for the people.

In June 1928, Goss told the State Grange at its 40th annual session in Chehalis that the PUD issue would not be on the ballot that year. His announcement did not explain that eleven Grangers serving in the Legislature advised against seeking a statewide vote for public power in November 1928. Instead he discussed a choice in procedure. He did not mention the conventional initiative route, nor did he see much chance of introducing the bill in an unfriendly Legislature. So he came down to the as yet untried method of an initiative to the Legislature. The Grange delegates agreed. Goss also made clear the need to raise from $1,500 to $5,000 for the campaign.

Not the least of the factors that made possible even the hope for enactment of the PUD initiative was the foresight of the Washington State Grange in winning the initiative, referendum and recall legislation in 1912.

Goss appeared before the 41st annual session in Spokane in June 1929 to report that the initiative was filed with the secretary of state October 25, 1928, and was certified to both houses of the Legislature. The Senate in February 1929 voted against the initiative 20 to 17. This automatically placed the initative on the ballot for November 1930, giving the Grange 20 months for the campaign.

One can only surmise that Goss was biding his time until he felt there was a chance to win. He could not win in the climate of the 1928 election that sent Herbert Hoover to the White House. But then came the stock market crash of October 1929 and the bankruptcy of a large electric utility holding company on November 2, 1929, all of which indicated that the pillars of finance had a hollow sound. Many people lost their life savings as one after another of the public utility holding companies went bankrupt in the 1929 to 1932 period.

The Federal Trade Commission's investigation of public utility holding companies and the monthly reports to the U.S. Senate over the seven years, 1928 to 1935, provided the nation's press and magazines with a continuing story of financial manipulation and profiteering to the detriment of the American public. The added investigation into utility propaganda activities had a major impact on public opinion. As the 1930 elections came nearer, many candidates took a stand in opposition to the improper practices of the private

Fred J. Chamberlain

utilities.

In urging Grangers to gird for battle, Goss told them in June 1929, "Every means that ingenuity can devise and money can employ will be used to defeat this measure." He especially called for speakers and a plan for training them. Finally he urged, "It is time to begin now."

That the campaign for the PUD initiative would be a battle royal was apparent from the dirty tricks employed by the private utilities to stop the effort to get signatures on the petitions in 1928. Fred Chamberlain wrote the history of the public power fight for the Grange's 50th Jubilee and it was printed June 10, 1939, as one-and-a-half pages of *The Grange News*. His is a ringside-seat report, quoting from his history:

"The Grange opened headquarters in the Railway Exchange Building in Seattle, with A.W. Swigart of Yakima, Helen Dahl of Seattle and Fred J. Chamberlain of Puyallup in charge. We were fully convinced that there should be aggressive action. We were also aware that we would be subjected to all kinds of deceptions and trickery because such tactics had been the experience of J.D. Ross in his campaigns (at Seattle City Light).

"We soon found our office was raided nearly every night; so we took all our signed petitions and important papers down to safety deposit boxes. Some solicitors came in and volunteered to circulate petitions, but took the filled ones to the power company, who copied them off, kept the originals and returned the duplicates to us, thus making them useless. This is only a sample of what happened during the whole campaign period."

The year 1930 brought Grangers to Wenatchee for their 42nd annual session. Goss discussed the Power Bill campaign at length. He anticipated that the private utilities would focus on the tax issue, since the PUD initiative did not require PUDs to pay taxes, until amended in 1941. Goss called for a low key campaign:

"The initiative measure is merely an enabling act. Its passage would not create a single power district or change the present power or tax situation in the slightest degree. It would merely authorize the people in the rural sections to call an election, should they desire, and decide for themselves whether they wished to form a public utility district or not. The people of our incorporated cities and towns have long enjoyed this right, and because of it have had good power service. The people of the country ask nothing more, nor nothing less than the people of our cities now have. They merely ask the right to decide this question for themselves. In all fairness I would ask for any just reason why the people of the rural sections are not as capable to decide this question for themselves as the people of our cities. Are we less intelligent? Are we less honest? That is the real issue and we challenge the power companies to justify the discrimination."

And as he had done for seven years, Goss warned Grangers that the ownership and control of Washington's water power was at stake.

For the report on what happened on the day before the election Chamberlain's brief 1939 history says this:

"Long before election time approached in 1930, one of the largest power companies announced it would take no active part against the proposed bill, as it was merely a matter for the taxpayers to decide. How well they took 'no active part' in the campaign was demonstrated when the night before election they employed about 400 people to distribute circulars all over Seattle stating that if the Power Bill passed, City Light would be taken over and the city would lose control. This last-minute trick was effective, because it resulted in losing the Seattle vote by about 16,000.

"This was a dismal surprise, because in a city loyal to public ownership, backed by the City Light Department, the Federation of Labor and many progresssive organizations, a good majority was anticipated.

"Election night we were full of gloom. The next morning it looked like certain defeat. By noon it was about a tie, but showing a steady

The Grange News was one of the prominent voices urging passage of Initiative No. 1 in 1930. This cartoon appeared on the eve of the election.

increase; so when the final vote was all in, we had carried the state by about 22,000 majority, and joy reigned supreme."

At the 43rd annual session in Bellingham in 1931 Goss hailed the PUD election victory, noting the series of private utility rate reductions, and he called attention to the possibility of federal hydroelectric projects. Mainly he felt that the Grange should take the lead in helping to form PUDs where this might be economically sound. He seemed to think that very few PUDs would be needed since the private utilities were cutting rates.

Public Power Hall of Fame Needed. The Public Power Hall of Fame for the state of Washington should always list Fred J. ("Dad") Chamberlain (1857-1948), "workhorse of the Grange." His cause was public ownership of electricity and he pursued this dream during 30 years on the Grange legislative committee (1917-1947) and 15 years on the Grange executive committee (1928-1943). He helped write the PUD law and promoted it.

Born September 13, 1857, in Schnerus, N.Y., he was educated in Iowa and served as editor. In 1885 he married Emma B. Thomas, who later became an invalid. He came West in 1889, taught at Buckley three years, was superintendent at Hoquiam four years, studied mineralogy at Washington State College two years, and in 1900 set up a berry and fruit farm near Puyallup. In 1910, he helped organize the Puyallup Grange and served as its first master. He organized 22 Granges during 1910-1936. His fiery pen often attacked the trusts and corruption. He died January 17, 1948.

The Great Depression. The public power issue dominated the 11-year Goss era because many farmers either had no power or had poor electric service at high rates.

Much energy was expended in rebuilding Grange membership in the six years from 1926 to 1931, when the number of Granges increased from 271 to 389 and members from 12,879 to 24,122. Losses followed in 1932 and 1933, dropping to 22,594, but the number of Granges increased to 420. Super Deputies Waters and Shea were the stalwart organizers.

The Great Depression brought massive unemployment. But the statistics understated the extent of poverty. The agricultural depression that began in 1921 continued for 20 years until 1941. In the rural areas many people lived at or close to the subsistence level. Wages everywhere were very low. Many jobs were part-time. The statistics counted the nonagricultural, civilian work force; farmers generally were not counted. Crops often went unsold and rotted in the field while the poor people of the cities did without adequate food.

The farmers had to struggle to keep body and soul together. Paying Grange dues was not always easy. Yet gradually the $4,700 deficit of 1922 became a $7,000 carry-over in 1931. Goss was a stickler for getting the financial house in order.

Finally, the Great Depression brought new management to the White House with the election of Franklin D. Roosevelt. He would soon call upon Goss to help solve some of the problems of the farmers.

But first, Washington State Master Goss had a request to make of the president. Accompanied by U.S. Senator Clarence Dill from Spokane on April 17, 1933, Goss went to the White House to urge construction of Grand Coulee Dam. Roosevelt, himself a member of the Grange, finally agreed to earmark $60 million when legislation and appropriations permitted. Dill obtained the enabling language in the bill.

Farm Banker. At the 45th annual session of the State Grange in Yakima June 6-9, 1933, Goss announced that he was not a candidate for reelection. President Roosevelt had asked him to become a commissioner of the newly established Farm Credit Administration, and he had accepted. A farewell address, his longest Master's Address, totaled 50 pages.

He used the occasion not only to report that the Washington State Grange was again in good health, but also to give some parting advice. He reported on the increased efficiency and effectiveness of the Grange headquarters office which he had initiated when he changed jobs from manager of Grange Wholesale to the position of master. He was the first master to have an office that was not in his home. His first small office was in space provided by Grange Wholesale. This was enlarged in rented space as the Grange secretary and *Grange News* were brought into the headquarters. He recommended that the lecturer be next moved to headquarters. He recommended a stronger deputy force as the key to Grange membership. He urged support for the various Grange cooperatives. And, finally, he suggested a better salary for the master and that the position should be a full-time job.

Most of his address, however, concerned the depressed farm prices and what Roosevelt might do about it. Mainly, he discussed new banking legislation and then his favorite subject—farm credit. Under the heading Farm Credit Administration he explained:

"Throughout our history, agriculture has been the victim of an unsound and greedy system of mortgage and bank credits. Brother C.B.

Kegley, former master of the Washington State Grange, led a fight for farm mortgage reform which culminated in the enactment of the Federal Farm Loan Act 17 years ago. Through it was established the world's greatest cooperative farm mortgage institution, but Congress provided an unsound privately-owned system of mortgage finance in the same measure."

Goss contended that special privileges which the act gave to private banks were not available to the Federal Land Banks in dealing with the local cooperative associations of farmers. Because the system had been failing for a dozen years, President Roosevelt created the Farm Credit Administration headed by Henry Morgenthau Jr. as governor. Serving with him as a board would be the five commissioners, each heading one of the main divisions. Initially Goss was selected to head the production loan division but when the more difficult job of farm land commissioner opened, Goss was drafted for the job and he would soon become widely known as the Land Bank Commissioner.

He held the position seven years, until 1940. Always he insisted on the cooperative approach with its advantages of decentralization and local control. He felt that the federal role should be mainly one of supervision rather than control.

His chief contribution in the new 1933 legislation was to amend the Intermediate Credit Act of 1923 so that the Federal Reserve Board could not terminate short-term production loans as it did in helping to bring on the 1921 depression.

Also among the 1933 amendments which he helped write was the "normal" value or price concept. Congress knew that at the then current values of farm produce, the farmer could not repay. The assumption was that the Agricultural Adjustment Administration (the Triple A or AAA of the same law) would produce the higher prices by reducing the surplus production. The assumption was wrong, because AAA did fail.

Early in 1940, a presidential campaign year, the pressure was on to provide outright subsidies, and writing down loans. Goss called it "abolition of personal responsibility" which would place the burden on fellow farm members of the cooperatives. Goss felt that farm credit should not be confused with the separate and more important issue of farm price parity. With normal farm prices, he felt, the farmers could repay their loans. Goss protested in vain and finally resigned.

His personal explanation is documented in a six-page letter to Washington State Grange News Editor Ted Berry dated March 14, 1940, which creates two impressions. The USDA has failed to solve the farm price parity problem, and Goss in effect was forced to resign for doing a good job. Moreover Washington Grangers and members of the National Grange sided with Goss.

Goss Becomes National Master. In his first State Master's Address of 1923, Goss gave credit to the National Grange for paying most of the expense of litigation to stop Bouck's use of the name "Grange" for his rebel organization. The National Grange also provided a Grange organizer for six months. The Goss policy was conciliatory.

From 1924 to 1933, Goss served on the executive committee of the National Grange, the last four years as chairman. He was the first Washington Granger to hold a significant office in the National Grange.

Then, while in effect on leave from the Grange, his duties as Commissioner of the Farm Credit Administration enabled him to be most helpful in providing credit to farmers. From the time he testified in 1916 for the Federal Farm Loan Act, he served a 25-year apprenticeship that led to his election as master of the National Grange in November 1941.

That was just two weeks before Pearl Harbor. He served in innumerable ways to help lead farmers to increase food production and to assist in the war effort. Significantly in those days of gasoline rationing, Grangers attended Grange meetings more regularly because of the many benefits from the meetings and because longer trips were precluded by the shortage of gasoline.

As national master he continued to provide leadership for strong farm cooperatives and a healthy farm credit system. A strong deputy program increased Grange membership.

A major accomplishment was the 1943 purchase of the National Grange Building property for $292,000 at 744 Jackson Place N.W, only a block from the White House. The eight-story building was renovated. Income from tenants paid for the building cost, thus basically giving the Grange a free home and a good investment. When this building was taken over by the U.S. Government in 1958, the Grange received the present site at 1616 H Street N.W. and funds to build the present 10-story home of the National Grange. President Eisenhower dedicated it June 29, 1960.

Goss' main wartime and postwar problem was the fight for parity of farm prices. He favored sound loan programs and opposed subsidies. He favored decentralized administration and local control. Although he did not support the Brannan Plan, in 1949 Secretary of Agriculture Brannan appointed him to the Agricultural Research

Policy Committee because of Goss' keen interest in research. An article on Goss in a 1945 issue of *Current Biography* closes, "Farm credit remains his pet subject; subsidies are his main gripe."

The Goss Legacy. Wherever Goss went, he left things stronger. He revived, rebuilt and left the Washington State Grange stronger. He helped rewrite national farm credit legislation and left that program stronger. Likewise, he served with distinction as master of the National Grange and left it stronger. He was a renaissance man bridging the gap between the old and the new.

In the evolution of Grange philosophy, he tried to pursue progressive goals by conservative means. He believed in pay as you go or other evidence of sound finance.

In helping enact the Washington PUD law he built better than he knew. Coupled with Columbia River development and rural electrification, the PUDs helped make Washington state a better place to live and work.

When he died October 25, 1950, Goss had ready on his desk the Master's Address for the November 15 opening of the National Grange. He said this about the Grangers who had passed on:

"Time rolls on. Our working years are few, and year by year we pass on our responsibilities to a new generation. It is Nature's way. May it be said of us, as we say today of those whose memory we now honor, that life for those we leave is a little brighter, a little easier, and a little better because we have lived."

CHAPTER NINE

KING: 1933 - 1941

DEVELOPING CO-OP ENTERPRISE

"We must all hang together, or assuredly we shall all hang separately."

Benjamin Franklin, 1776,
at the signing of the
Declaration of Independence

By March 1933, the Great Depression had deepened to the point of near paralysis. The stock market crash of October 1929 dried up sources of funds, drastically slowed investments, closed factories and put people out of work. Four million were unemployed in 1930, eight million in 1931, 12 million in 1932, and 13 million by 1933 when one in four workers was unemployed. Corn at 10 cents a bushel could not pay the cost of transportation; it was widely burned as a fuel in the farm kitchen stove. City people sorted garbage to find food. Every city had its soup lines. Banks were closing.

In his inaugural address of March 4, 1933, Franklin Roosevelt warned against fear of fear itself and asked for a national consecration to the tasks ahead. He called a special session of Congress for March 9 and Congress on that day passed the Emergency Banking Act.

In 100 days the Congress adopted 15 laws. It established the Tennessee Valley Authority. It enacted the National Industrial Recovery Act (N.I.R.A.), which created the Works Progress Administration (WPA) with $3.3 billion to fund public works—including Grand Coulee and Bonneville dams. The Congress passed the Civilian Conservation Act, six laws relating to banking and finance, and three laws for agriculture. The Agricultural Adjustment Act (A.A.A.), dedicated mainly to reducing crop surpluses, was later declared unconstitutional. The Emergency Farm Mortgage Act provided for refinancing farm mortgages. The third was the Farm Credit Act, which Goss helped write and would soon help to administer. Goss explained the three new farm laws in his Master's Address June 1933 at Yakima. This was the climate as the Washington State Grange elected its eighth state master.

Ervin E. King (1894-1941) was born in Davenport, Washington, graduated from Washington State College in 1917 and married

Ervin E. King

Maybelle Robinson in 1918. They had a son and a daughter.

He became a wheat farmer near Pullman in 1926. He was a member of Mondovi Grange in Lincoln County and then of Whelan Grange in Whitman County, serving as master. He organized nine Granges. In June 1933 he was elected State Grange master, serving until his death in 1941.

The eight-year King era was marked by activities, progress and accomplishments on six major fronts. First, the Washington State Grange membership soared from 22,000 to 37,000. Second, important farm legislation passed including the Bone Power Bill to permit cities to serve rural areas; the blanket primary bill to allow all voters to vote on all candidates; and an "in-lieu" tax on PUD electricity sales to replace local taxes formerly paid by a private utility. Third, the State Grange headquarters was built and dedicated in 1935. Fourth, the Grange fought on a broad front for low cost power resulting in voter approval for forming, ultimately, 31 PUDs. Fifth, celebration of the Grange's 50th anniversary in 1939 provided an opportunity for a mid-century review of Grange progress. Sixth, and in King's opinion most important, was the surge in Grange cooperative activity.

Increase in Membership. Many circumstances influence the rise and fall in Grange membership. On occasion, and contrary to what might be expected, the membership has grown in hard times and dropped in good times. A more reliable guide is that new members tend to come in when the Grange is promoting legislation, such as the PUD law, or is offering a service, such as those of the Grange cooperatives.

The rise in membership during the King era reflects the efforts of the deputies and especially of the two "Super Deputies," Frank P. Waters and Ira E. Shea. Waters (1855-1936), who incidentally was a telegrapher friend of Thomas Edison, came to Washington in 1901, settling in Stevens County. He had a fiery enthusiasm for the Grange. From 1915 to 1935 "Dad" Waters organized 92 Granges, starting under Kegley and into the early years under King. Shea (1895-1987) was trained by Waters as he reports in his 1983 book, *The Grange Was My Life*. Shea organized a record 135 Granges from 1925 to

Ira E. Shea

Frank P. Waters

Washington Grange members took pride in owning the first state Grange headquarters in the nation. In this picture, taken in 1939, only two floors are seen. The top story of the building was added later.

1942. His peak years were 22 Granges formed in 1930 and 18 in 1934. He was State Grange lecturer from 1939 to 1946 and received the Grange leadership award in 1964. From reading his book one can identify two factors that may have enabled him to reach age 92. He had a good sense of humor and he was full of praise for all of the good Grange cooks. In a sense, his is a "good cook" book.

The depression years of 1934 and 1935 brought on a boom in Grange membership. The membership stood at 22,594 at the end of 1933 and was up 60 percent to 36,741 in 1941. The two big gains were 6,540 in 1934, an all-time record, and 4,974 in 1935, which is the third highest year of record. There was a slight drop in 1940.

Despite the poverty, and possibly in part because of the hard times, many people joined the Grange. There were many causes. The fight for the blanket primary took place in 1934 and 1935. Grange Insurance Association launched its revolving funds in 1935. The rising optimism was an influence as work started on Grand Coulee and Bonneville dams. Goss had rebuilt the Grange and left a favorable record; he continued to help as Federal Land Bank commissioner. The big, new Washington State Grange headquarters building made a good impression. The many promotion campaigns for forming PUDs involved people in all counties. The growing Grange cooperatives also involved many people and promised some savings. Not the least of the influences was the Goss legacy. The Grange was a smooth-running organization reflecting a spirit of friendliness and competence in getting things done.

The last Washington county to form a Grange was Columbia County in 1935, which illustrates a point. To be truly a statewide agency the Grange must be active in every county. Experience has shown that the Grange can be especially valuable and useful in the smaller and remote counties, where farmers often feel that they are overlooked.

Legislative Efforts Succeed. Washington had enacted the direct primary largely through the leadership of Kegley in 1907 in building a coalition of rural and urban groups. Wisconsin had pioneered the direct primary in 1903 under the leadership of Robert M. LaFollette.

In 1934, the Washington State Grange submitted the blanket primary initiative to the Legislature; it was enacted in 1935. The blanket primary is a single ballot listing all candidates with party affiliation shown. All voters can vote on all candidates.

In 1933, the Legislature approved the Bone Power Bill, enabling municipal electric systems to sell electricity outside the city limits. Private utilities had this law referred to the people and in 1934 Washington voters approved the Bone Bill.

The third major legislative change was the PUD "in-lieu" tax. The 1930 PUD initiative did not include a tax on electricity sold by PUDs. The PUDs and the Grange asked the Legislature in 1941 to enact a gross electric revenue tax on PUD sales. The purpose was to replace the local property taxes formerly paid by a private utility on an electric system taken over by a PUD. The Legislature agreed.

A Home for Washington State Grange. King particularly enjoyed dedicating a new Grange hall. His Master's Addresses list the dedications in each year. There is something about the planning and building of a Grange hall that makes for a stronger, more stable Grange. It may be the kind of spirit that goes into a barn raising. Sometimes non-Grangers want to help because to them it is really a community center. Grange halls are used in so many, many ways.

The need for a Washington State Grange headquarters building had long been apparent to Albert Goss. Starting in 1922 he moved his office in the Associated Grange Warehouse Company where he had been manager. As master, he had a separate office which became the State Grange headquarters. It was rental space and several moves followed, always in rented, crowded space.

King recommended in 1934 that the Grange should buy or build, and the members agreed. The executive committee surveyed the situation and worked out a plan for centralizing Grange activities under one roof. In the spring of 1935 a lot was purchased near the Seattle waterfront (west of the present location of the Space Needle, built for the 1962 World's Fair). Ground was broken March 2, construction started March 11 and the building completed May 10, five days ahead of schedule. On May 10, the Washington State Grange moved into the only state headquarters building in the nation. The two-story, reinforced concrete, fireproof building was 60 feet by 110 feet, providing 13,000 square feet at a cost of $30,000. Provision was made for a third story, which was added later. The cost was shared by the Grange Printing Cooperative, Grange Cooperative Wholesale, Washington Fire Relief, Grange Powder Co. and *The Grange News*. King gives the main credit for the building to Fred Chamberlain.

Not the least of the important effects of the building was confirmation of the Goss recommendation that the master serve on a full-time basis. This soon applied to the secretary and lecturer as well.

Public Power Fight Continues. Enactment of the PUD initiative in 1930 was only the beginning.

In 1932, people of eight counties voted on whether to form PUDs. Private utility opposition was fierce with their most effective argument being that the PUD law made no provision for paying taxes. Five PUDs were voted down and the three partials were approved but were absorbed by later countywide PUDs.

In 1934, four PUDs were voted in, Franklin and Benton countywide and Mason No. 1 and Mason No. 3. The first PUD to begin operation was Mason No. 1 in 1935. Also in 1935 the State Supreme Court validated the PUD law.

The big surge of public power sentiment came in 1936 when 15 PUDs were voted in: Chelan, Douglas, Ferry, Kittitas, Lewis, Lincoln, Okanogan, Pacific No. 2, Pend Oreille, Skagit, Snohomish, Stevens, Wahkiakum, Whatcom and Cowlitz.

Fred Chamberlain called a meeting of all PUD commissioners in Seattle, December 7, 1936, to establish the Washington Public Utility Commissioners Association. The name was changed in 1952 to Washington Public Utility Districts Association. The author attended the PUD association's 50th anniversary celebration Dec. 10-11, 1986 in Seattle. For 50 years the relationships of the PUD Association and Washington State Grange have been close.

The construction of Grand Coulee and Bonneville dams led Oregon and Washington leaders to propose statewide public transmission systems. At the 1936 elections the proposals were rejected. That narrowed the power transmission choice to private power or federal. The Grange helped decide the issue in favor of a federal transmission system.

In 1937, Oregon and Washington State Granges both supported the bill that became the Bonneville Project Act. At a joint meeting early in 1937 the two State Granges agreed to submit testimony favoring a regional federal transmission system with power to be sold at wholesale on a postage stamp or uniform rate basis. President Roosevelt signed the Bonneville Project Act on August 20, 1937. This created the Bonneville Power Administration to build federal lines and market power from Bonneville Dam. F.D.R. visited the Northwest to dedicate Bonneville Dam on September 28, 1937. On October 10, 1937, he named James Dalmage Ross, the longtime superintendent of Seattle City Light, as administrator of the Bonneville Power Administration. Later, BPA was authorized to market power from Grand Coulee and 28 other federal dams.

By accepting the appointment, Ross assumed leadership for the federal power program in the Northwest.

In four short years, 1933 to 1937, President Roosevelt had provided the leadership to put in place the major laws that made up the federal power program, and the Grange had supported that program. These major laws were the Tennessee Valley Authority Act of 1933, the Securities and Exchange Act of 1934, the Public Utility Act of 1935, the Rural Electrification Act of 1936 and the Bonneville Project Act of 1937. The Public Utility Act of 1935 included two laws. It rewrote and strengthened the Federal Water Power Act of 1920 renaming it the Federal Power Act and it enacted the Public Utility Holding Company Act. The latter was of great interest to the Northwest because virtually all private utilities in the region were owned by absentee holding companies. These laws constituted a major change in national policy, representing a mid-course correction for the 50-year old electric utility industry. The handling of the nation's electric power opportunity had become a matter of federal concern. After 50 years of laissez faire or hands off policy, the Congress had declared that the furnishing of electric service was hereafter to be regarded as a public utility responsibility affected with a public interest. The federal government made a basic shift from a passive role to an active approach.

The president and the Congress had also launched the building of dozens of large multiple purpose water power dams. The power from these dams was to be sold with preference to nonprofit, consumer-owned electric systems. The preference clause, which appears in some 30 enactments of laws and executive orders, has long had the support of the Washington State Grange.

The new PUDs would soon have an interest in these new laws. Several PUDs borrowed money from the Rural Electrification Administration. As the slow process began of breaking up the public utility holding companies, the PUDs were to make several efforts to buy the private utilities in Washington. They were unable to buy out any one of the three major companies as a whole, but the individual PUDs would later complete several dozen acquisitions of private utilities in their respective counties.

At the 1938 general election seven more PUDs were formed: Clark, Grays Harbor, Grant, Klickitat, San Juan, Skamania and Thurston. In 1940, four more were approved including Clallam, which is in the electric business; Kitsap and Jefferson, which are in the water business; and Yakima.

The 1940 election was hard fought. Four PUDs were voted down. Public ownership attempts in Portland and Spokane failed. The main effort concerned the private power sponsored Initiative 139 to require an election for each proposed PUD bond issue. It was defeated 362,508 to 253,318. The Grange, of course, was most active.

In fact, the Grange headquarters was the center for battle after battle in the many efforts to establish PUDs, favor or oppose legislation, and help finance court cases.

The last Grange effort on behalf of public power during the King era was the successful campaign of the Grange and the PUDs to sponsor legislation to place a gross revenue tax on PUD electricity sales. This was in lieu of property taxes formerly paid by private utilities on properties purchased by a PUD.

Washington's PUD pioneering involved three stages: The first was the enactment of the PUD initiative in 1930. The second stage was forming the individual PUDs. During the King era 30 PUDs were voted in starting in 1934 and ending in 1940. Asotin PUD was approved by the voters in 1984 and became the 31st PUD. The third stage would be that of getting into business. Some beginnings toward this end were made during the King era. Mason No. 1 began a very small operation in 1935. Lewis, Cowlitz and Mason No. 3 were in operation in 1939. Grays Harbor, Pacific, Skamania and Wahkiakum were operating in 1940.

Golden Jubilee. At the end of 1939 Grange membership stood at a record 37,004 in 488 Granges. The number of Granges had peaked in 1937 at 490. The membership of 36,428 that year resulted in an average of 74 members per Grange. After 1937 the actual number of Granges would gradually decline toward 400 but the members per Grange would more than double.

To celebrate the 50th birthday of the Washington State Grange, the June 10, 1939, *Grange News* came out with an all-time record issue in four sections. In addition to the usual 16-page issue, there were three other sections containing 40 pages of feature articles on the many activities and achievements of the Grange. There were also a number of good historical articles, including Fred Chamberlain's history of public power. The special edition pictured the Grange in terms of four functions: cooperation, education, legislation and recreation. These made up the four pillars of the Grange. The largest 16-page section was reserved for Master King's favorite subject, cooperatives.

Cooperatives Flourish. Since 1874, one of the purposes of the National Grange proposed "buying together, selling together, and in general, acting together for mutual protection."

In 1908, President Theodore Roosevelt's Country Life Commission noted the success of agricultural cooperatives in Europe, and recommended greater use of the cooperative idea in this country.

During the 1930s several U.S. delegations visited European cooperatives and reported their achievements. Marquis Childs' 1936 book *Sweden—The Middle Way* extolled the cooperative way of life in that country. The book went through a dozen printings.

Goss had laid down a good foundation of Grange cooperative management in the 1920s. King expanded the number of cooperative enterprises in the 1930s. The resulting success of the cooperatives also stimulated membership growth of the Grange.

The State Grange Cooperative Committee in 1939 adopted a resolution saying, "Cooperation is the cornerstone of the Grange." Cooperation to King meant forming farmer-owned cooperatives. The resolution goes on to suggest greater effort to provide knowledge of the cooperative movement, directs the state lecturer to emphasize study of cooperatives and urges each Grange to take part in education on cooperatives.

Cooperatives were flourishing. The Farm Credit Act of June 16, 1933, had rounded out the system of cooperative agricultural credit. Virtually all loans were to be available mainly through cooperatives. The Banks for Cooperatives were established to finance cooperatives. Two years later the Rural Electrification Act provided another large loan program for cooperatives. The Farmer Cooperative Ser-

The Grange Insurance Association, created in the barn below, has evolved over the years and now owns a contemporary office building (bottom) in downtown Seattle.

vice provided research and information on cooperatives.

In his farewell to the State Grange, written just before he died June 5, 1941, Ervin King concluded, "The greatest need in our country today is cooperation." It was the theme he had expressed in seven previous Master's Addresses, and almost half of each address reported on the progress of Grange cooperative enterprises.

The June 10, 1939, Jubilee issue of *The Grange News* provided a convenient summary of the eight cooperatives then sponsored by the Washington State Grange.

Grange Insurance Association is the oldest and largest in the Washington State Grange group of cooperative enterprises.

The old expression, "Were you born in a barn?" is part of the Horatio Alger story of GIA—it was born in a barn. The Washington State Grange held its fifth annual session in the new Jewett barn at White Salmon June 6-9, 1893. State Master D.L. Russell recommended forming a mutual fire insurance company to serve Washington Grangers. The delegates agreed and authorized a committee to proceed. A month later, on July 6, the five-man committee headed by Russell met in the same barn to draft the constitution and bylaws of the Washington Fire Relief Association. The name was changed in 1936 to Grange Fire Insurance Association and in 1943, reflecting the start of auto insurance, the name was shortened to Grange Insurance Association (GIA).

The leaders had been involved in the Lower Columbia Fire Relief Association, which was formed by the Oregon State Grange in 1884 and went into business in 1886. It operated by means of the loss assessment method. The insured pays in a nominal premium to pay for the forms and incidental costs, and is then subject to an assessment when a loss occurs. Doubt had existed as to the legality of such assessments. The doubt continued to exist when the Washingtonians split off to form their own mutual insurance group. In an article in the June 10, 1939, issue of *The Grange News* Washougal pioneer Granger C.J. Moore explained that while he was in the Washington House and Augustus High in the Senate, they sponsored successful legislation making such assessments legal.

The newly organized Washington Fire Relief Association bylaws provided that when the sign-ups reached $100,000, the association would meet, elect directors and sign the policies. The goal was reached in April 1894 and the board was elected and took office on April 19, 1894, with Russell as president, serving to 1907, and Augustus High as secretary, serving to 1908. Jesse Wing became secretary in 1908 serving to 1915. Thus the first three state masters were actively involved.

It started as a shoestring operation with no full-time employees. It initially served almost entirely in Clark, Skamania, Klickitat and Cowlitz counties. By 1914, insurance in force reached $5 million, by 1919 it was at $7 million, by 1930 about $8 million tripling to $25 million in 1939.

Goss praised the association for its help to the Grange in the crisis of 1922 and 1923. He said it saved the Grange.

By 1928, the association hired a fire inspector to inspect premises for insurability.

Things began to move with the election of Charles F. Keiser of Chelan County in June 1929. He served as president for 25 years to 1954, then remained on the board to 1959, at which time he retired.

In August 1930, the association rented its first office space in Seattle's Kulien Building.

The foreclosures during the Depression and other losses forced the board to borrow $8,000 with each board member signing as surety. This led to incorporation on August 6, 1931.

In 1933, the association began insuring grain against fire. Also in that year the mutual was changed to a cooperative, which led to a 1935 decision to rotate the annual surplus as a dividend after five years. In 1938, the surplus of 1933 was paid out. Actually it was paid early in 1939 and amounted to $21,000.

In 1935, the board authorized Secretary P.J. Cleaver to hire a young man as a trainee. He selected Frank McCartney, who would become GIA's secretary 1945 to 1956, and then, from 1972 to 1987, State Grange secretary.

The subject of debate during 1939 to 1941 was whether to insure automobiles. The decision in 1941 was to go ahead, but no auto insurance was put into effect until 1946.

In 1951, GIA was invited by Oregon State Grange to offer automobile insurance in Oregon. In the late 1950s similar arrangements were offered in Wyoming, Montana, Idaho and Colorado. But both Idaho and Colorado had their own fire insurance companies, so in those two states GIA initially offered only liability and automobile insurance. In 1963, GIA by invitation offered fire insurance in California. In time the Grange fire insurance programs in Colorado and California merged into GIA. As a result, GIA is the largest of the regional insurers serving farmers in the West.

Grange Cooperative Wholesale was the most visible of the eight Grange cooperatives as of 1939. The numerous Grange stores and warehouses, bulk petroleum storage tanks and tanker trucks could

Grange Supply stores, scattered throughout Washington, started in Almira. The local units marketed most items needed by rural residents but petroleum products eventually became the cooperative's biggest sellers.

be seen in almost all counties. Organized in 1918 as Grange Wholesale Warehouse Company, the initial goal was to combine the purchasing power of the 50 or more small Grange cooperative supply units by means of centralized purchasing. R.I. Case was manager until Goss was selected in 1920. Goss instituted a centralized bookkeeping and auditing system, insisted on cash transactions and concentrated on getting a good credit rating. For a time GWWC had to borrow money from the Grange. A.E. Shearer served as manager 1922-24, P.J. Cleaver until 1925 (later with GIA), and W.O. Dickinson was still manager in 1939. J.G. Wetter became auditor in 1921.

The main expansion of the 1930s was into petroleum, which soon was half of the business, amounting to 8,000,000 gallons in 1936. Lincoln County Pomona Master Henry P. Carstensen promoted the first petroleum contract at the Almira store in 1931. Ervin E. King promoted the Pullman unit. By the end of 1933 there were 19 bulk fuel storage plants in eastern Washington and one near Tacoma.

A Grange cooperative deputy, William T. Smith of Wheatland, also Whitman Pomona master, was appointed in 1934 to promote new supply units and maintain contact with all supply units.

Grange Co-op Wholesale and the local warehouse units provided much opportunity for leadership training and business experience. State Grange Treasurer Fred Nelsen served on the board from the beginning. C.E. Flint, R.I. Case and A.E. Shearer were early board members. In the 1937 reorganization, the State Grange turned the control of the GCW over to the supply units who elected eight board members by districts, with State Grange appointing the ninth member. In 1937, GCW launched a monthly paper, *Grange Cooperative News*.

The 1938 report showed $3 million in sales and completion of many warehouse facilities. The Spokane branch had a warehouse 250 feet long.

In the next half century the trend for farm supply cooperatives has been one of consolidations and mergers. The renamed Grange Supply Stores survived largely because of affiliation with CENEX. Formed in 1931 as Farmers Union Central Exchange, CENEX emphasized the integrated ownership of oil wells and refineries as well as bulk handling facilities. As of 1986 CENEX reported 500,000 member-owners in 1,600 local cooperatives in 13 states and annual sales of $1.4 billion. Thus, Grange Supply/CENEX has survived despite many ups and downs.

The cooperatives organized by the Grange offered alternative sources of supply for members, often at substantial savings. The Columbia County Grange Supply store in Dayton, below, boasted a grocery section featuring several brands of popular breakfast cereals.

Grange Powder Company was formed in 1925 to produce stumping powder to dynamite stumps at a reasonable cost. Initially, surplus powder from the government was used. In 1934, the company purchased the patent rights and built a plant to produce stumping powder as a finished product. It was a safe, slow-acting superior powder. The plant was near Issaquah and employed six to nine men. It produced a ton per eight-hour shift but could easily be expanded. Early in 1941, part of the plant was dedicated to fertilizer production as a second product. Grange Powder Company ceased operations during World War II and sold its plant.

Grange Mutual Life Company was incorporated in Idaho in 1934, and began doing life insurance business in both Idaho and Washington in 1935, Oregon in 1940 and Montana in 1941. By the end of 1940 the policyholders had an equity of $55,000. By 1987 GML had grown into a healthy enterprise with assets of over $150 million.

Grange Milling Company was organized in 1935 to acquire the Big Bend Milling Co. plant at Davenport in Lincoln County. It included a five-story reinforced concrete mill and related buildings. The mill was refurbished and improved. The State Grange home economics department helped to promote sales for the high quality flour produced, known as the Pomona brand.

When the mill was gutted by fire October 28, 1939, the members promptly rebuilt. The insurance paid off the mortgage and financed the rebuilding. Operations resumed in September 1940. In 1951 the cooperative was purchased locally by farmers in Lincoln County.

Grange Cooperative Livestock Marketing Association was organized in October 1938 after years of study by Grange livestock marketing committees. A former county agent from Idaho, P.R. Gladhart, was named manager. The staff included a salesman and bookkeeper.

GCLMA operated as a commission firm at Spokane's Old Union Stockyards but provided many services in addition to selling livestock for some 800 farmers. It sorted and assembled animals, located feeders and provided information on freight rates, market prices and conditions.

The rapid success of the eastern Washington operation led to buying a site for establishing a stockyards at Auburn and this effort was moving ahead in 1941, gradually overcoming obstacles.

The Auburn yard was sold in 1945 and the association was soon disbanded.

Grange Cooperative Printing Association was established at the end of 1938, as the baby of Grange co-ops. First proposed in 1935, it was approved by the members on the argument that just the printing for various Grange organizations would enable the plant to break even. By 1941 the company was doing printing for eleven organizations. The printing company was still operating successfully in 1986 when it was sold and renamed Valco Graphics.

The Grange News was started in 1912 as the *Agricultural Grange News*. Predecessor publications were *Grange Bulletin*,1905-1907, and *The Pacific Grange Bulletin*, jointly with Oregon, 1908-1912. The name change to *The Grange News* came in 1927. State Grange Secretary Fred W. Lewis (1907-1937) filled in as editor several times from 1909 to 1927. John M. (Jack) Eisen was employed in 1927 to sell advertising and he became advertising manager in 1930. Always the aim was to make *The Grange News* self-supporting.

Ted F. Berry became editor in 1935, serving 38 years until he died in 1973. Avis Beam joined Grange News in 1936. She was in her 50th year with the Grange when she retired in November 1985.

The Grange News in 1988 was in its 77th year as the voice of the Washington State Grange.

Cooperating with Others. Washington State Grange created cooperatives only when a need existed and was not being satisfactorily met. The Grange cooperated with poultry and egg cooperatives, dairy, wheat, cattle and other commodity groups. The Grange believed as King said, "The greatest need in our country is cooperation."

CHAPTER TEN

CARSTENSEN:
1941-1953

BUILDING THE GRANGE IN WAR AND PEACE

"There's a long, long trail awinding
Into the land of my dreams
Where the nightingales are singing
And a white moon beams.

"There's a long, long night of waiting
Until my dreams all come true;
'Til the day when I'll be going down
That long, long trail with you."

Stoddard King
From a favorite Grange song.

With the death of Ervin King a few days before the 52nd annual session at Ellensburg, June 10-13, 1941, the Washington State Grange elected Henry P. Carstensen, its overseer of the past eight years, as the ninth state master. The dark clouds of war were looming on the horizon.

Henry P. Carstensen (1894-1967) served for 12 years from 1941 to 1953. He was born May 9, 1894, in Schleswig-Holstein of Danish-German parents. At 14 he was in Almira in Lincoln County working on a wheat farm. He began growing wheat in 1912, eventually farming 2,200 acres; became a citizen at 21 in 1915; attended Wenatchee Business College; and in 1916 married Elizabeth Blinn. They had three children.

The Carstensens celebrated their 50th anniversary in 1966. He died August 17, 1967. He was a member of Grand Coulee Grange No. 807, and served there as master.

Goss appointed him as a deputy, he was Lincoln Pomona master four years, served as State overseer throughout the King era of 1933-1941, and organized nine Granges between 1929 and 1941.

Carstensen pioneered the first petroleum contract for the Almira Grange store in 1931, thus launching Grange Cooperative Wholesale in the lucrative petroleum business. He was an active overseer, serving on the executive, legislative and cooperative committees. When GIA was divided on the issue, he promoted auto insurance. He was an organizer and served on the board of Grange Cooperative Livestock Marketing Association. He had served his apprenticeship in advancing Grange programs.

Turbulence marked the years 1941 to 1953. The world would never be the same. Human beings and nations were swept along by the need to win World War II, then by the four years of conversion toward an elusive peace before plunging into the Korean war of 1950 to 1953.

Grand Coulee and Bonneville dams strained to provide power for building ships and producing aluminum for airplanes. While their sons went off to war, Grangers flexed their muscles to produce record crops to feed the world.

Added jobs resulted in a dramatic growth in the state's population. Some war industries, mainly the Boeing Company, aluminum plants and the Hanford nuclear complex continued to grow in war and peace. Irrigation water from Grand Coulee Dam finally came to the Columbia Basin Project, changing the desert into an oasis of green crops. Washington State Grange membership increased over 30 percent, passing the 50,000 member mark.

A PUD is a paper tiger, until it gets into business. During this 12-

Henry P. Carstensen

year period most PUDs became operational. In 1947, the notorious 80th Congress tried to abolish the federal power program. In 1948, the people voted against the misguided policies of the 80th Congress.

The Grange Insurance Association, Grange Mutual Life Company and Grange Cooperative Wholesale enjoyed steady growth and financial strength. Some business ventures of the Grange peaked out and diminished. When the war put an end to sources of stumping powder, the Grange Powder Company was promptly dissolved and its assets sold.

Membership Growth Mirrors the Grange. Membership growth is both cause and result. It can cause Grangers to launch a public interest campaign or add a service that helps the farmer and the public. It can result in attracting non-Grangers to become members.

The membership at the end of 1941 stood at 36,741 and rose each year for seven years. The peak gains were 5,943 in 1944, the second greatest annual increase in Washington. Next year the gain of 4,415 was the fourth highest. Thus the two years of heaviest war fighting in 1944 and 1945 swelled the ranks of Washington Grangers by 10,358. The 50,000 mark was passed in 1946. The seven year total gain was 18,084. One major factor in this surge was the availability of GIA's auto insurance approved in 1941 and starting in 1946.

The reverse trend began in 1949 with a net loss of 1,585 and smaller losses each year to a final count of 50,894 at the end of 1953. This amounts to an overall net rise in the Carstensen period of 14,153. Importantly, the average size of Granges 1941-53 rose from 76 to 106 members, first exceeding 100 in 1945.

The war years brought Grangers closer together and brought many new people into the ranks. The rationing of tires and gasoline may have helped. Much greater was the feeling that we are all in this thing together and, as mentioned earlier, GIA auto insurance attracted new members.

The years of decline may have reflected a general postwar reaction and some disillusionment over the failure to achieve a meaningful peace. Internally, within the Granges, two controversies may have been partially responsible for the loss of some members.

Washington Gains Population. During the 1940 decade Washington gained 642,772 people to reach 2,378,963 in the 1950 census. This compares to only 594,201 gained in the previous 30 years. Washington's 37 percent population growth in the 1940s compares to the national average of 14.5 percent. Four states lost population during the1940s; others just held their own. California, however, gained over 50 percent, and Oregon grew 40 percent. The robust Washington growth was due mainly to the attraction of shipyard and aircraft production, and other defense activities. Many people were eager to jump at the opportunity offered by war production jobs; they paid reasonably well. To people in the high plains states, the memories of the dust bowl storms and harsh climate also provided incentive to move to Washington. Later in the 1940s, the opening of lands in the Columbia Basin Project brought some people. Finally, the publicity surrounding the building of Bonneville and Grand Coulee dams and electricity for everybody created a favorable climate. And, having come, they stayed after the war.

Grange During the War. Over the years Grangers took a dim view of conscription in time of peace and excessive profits in time of war. Grangers also had bad memories of World War I and its disastrous aftermath for farmers and the nation. This time things would be different.

Carstensen's election as state master in June 1941 was followed by Albert Goss's election as national master in November, a few weeks before the bombing of Pearl Harbor. Goss had easy access to the White House and others in authority. He promptly advised Granges to maintain their regular meeting schedules and to support all community war activities including Red Cross, scrap drives, blood donations, war gardening and bond sales. Gas rationing discouraged long trips, but helped Grange attendance because it didn't take much gas to get to local Grange meetings. Attendance increased and the war efforts tended to unify Granges. Goss served on the labor-management policy committee of the War Manpower Commission.

The Grange News carried many stories on coping with the material shortages and other problems of war. Special issues of the newspaper came out at the end of the war, one in September, 1945, and the big 44-page issue of November 17, 1945.

These included photographs of about 200 Washington Grangers who died in the service of their country. Other stories chronicled the heroism and sacrifices.

When Grangers bought $700,000 in war bonds, they earned the right to sponsor a bomber honoring Lt. Col. Gregory (Pappy) Boyington, a Marine Ace from Okanogan. At that time the song "Pistol Packin' Mama" was popular, so Assistant Editor Avis Beam suggested "Pistol Packing Papa," and that is the name that soon flew off over enemy territory. A picture of the bomber appeared in the special issue of *The Grange News*.

A Vigorous Style. Carstensen was different. Perhaps as an immigrant boy he had learned to be up and doing while some might still just be thinking about it. He was decisive, forever optimistic and persistent. Physically he was not large but was trim and wiry, and seemingly full of energy. He could be peppery yet was ever ready with a friendly, infectious smile. He may have struck some as impatient, for he was an activist and a doer.

His Master's Addresses may have reflected the wartime plea to conserve paper. They ranged from eight and one-half to 23 pages. The entire proceedings in 1944 ran only 191 pages, and the executive committee made a major economy decision by not holding an annual session in 1945. The 1946 session was entitled the 56th and 57th annual session.

Carstensen was an innovator. The employment of John L. King as radio and research director was announced in 1943, and this became a permanent Grange function. By 1944, John L. King's radio program, "Meet the Grange," was being carried on 27 radio stations in Montana, Idaho and Oregon, as well as Washington. The aim was 104 programs per year, two each week.

Carstensen established the State Grange Agricultural Department in 1944 by naming Richard G. Hedges as full-time chairman of the Agricultural Committee.

He felt that was as far as the Grange could go, but that the need was really for a strong advocate for each commodity. That was an idea whose time would come much later, when the Grange successfully sponsored legislation authorizing agricultural commodity commissions, one for each major crop.

The state master has the assistance of officers, staff, deputies and committee members. A key member of Carstensen's team was Frieda Berger, state lecturer 1946-1955. She was born in Wisconsin in 1905 of a Swiss family of cheese makers which moved to Tekoa in 1910. She received a teaching certificate from Eastern College of Education in Cheney, taught in Ferry County during 1923 and joined the Grange, married Fred Berger 1927, returned to Tekoa 1933 and assisted in organizing Tekoa Grange No. 1011 in 1934. She served there in all key offices and as Whitman County Pomona lecturer and then secretary.

As state lecturer she worked closely with the Grange youth program and helped form the Washington State Youth Group, of which she became an honorary life member. She was instrumental in establishing the Grange talent program, the lecturer scroll, the lecturer achievement plaque and adoption of the Washington State Grange song. She became a member of the Historical Committee in

Frieda Berger

Charles Hodde

1975 and has been chairman since 1978. She received the Grange Leadership Award in 1980.

Junior Grange and Youth. As early as July 1868, Oliver Hudson Kelley expressed a desire for "an organization for the little folks." He also wrote Francis M. McDowell, another of the seven founders of the Grange, "I suggest having a primary degree expressly for the little folks from six or eight to 16 years, so as to entertain and instruct the children in the rural districts and get their minds interested in the study of the beauties of nature, as well as to afford them some rational recreation." At the 1877 National session, Kelley recommended, "Establish primary Granges for children. In these we can teach them by illustrative lessons, interspersed with music and singing, to love the farm. Give them amusement and recreation. Have in each Grange a microscope and a copy of Webster's Unabridged." Texas originated the juvenile Grange (now called junior Grange) in 1888, and in 1890 the National Grange adopted the idea and ritual. Washington's first was Felida Juvenile Grange No. 1 in 1907.

In 1943, Carstensen deplored the net loss of five juvenile Granges and decided to do something about it. In 1944, he named Lena Lloyd as full-time state juvenile matron, and in 1946 her results were apparent for all to see. The number of juvenile Granges had jumped from 56 to 89, and membership rose from 963 to 2,425. She was followed by Bernice Wilson and Frances Anderson. The 1953 roster showed 106 juvenile Granges.

From 1945 to 1948 Elizabeth Carstensen, wife of the state master, served as National Grange juvenile matron.

In the past 40 years Washington State Grange has adopted a wide range of activities and contests for young people. These activities are sponsored by three Grange departments—junior, youth and lecturer—and are listed each year in the *Handbook* of the Washington State Grange.

The junior directors, a couple, work through seven district directors in conducting the Grange camping program and the many contests. The State Grange Junior Committee consists of the state and district directors. Junior Grangers are age five to 14.

The state youth director and seven district directors comprise the State Grange Youth Committee, which conducts the many youth activities and contests. Eligibility ages for the contests vary, thus the outstanding young adult must be 21 to 35 inclusive. The young couple of the year must each be under 35.

The 1986 Roster shows 39 junior Granges in Washington with from eight to 35 members, but eight do not report members.

Getting into the Power Business. While a few were already operating, most of the newly formed PUDs were taking steps to get into business when the U.S. entered World War II. The Bonneville Power Administration had helped several PUDs to get started by supplying them with wholesale power, but now the serving of defense loads had priority. It looked like public power would be on ice for the duration of the war.

Carstensen saw no reason for waiting. Moreover, he was suspicious of the private power argument that we should wait until the boys' return after the war. With Grange moral support the PUD commissioners filed condemnation suits to acquire the electric distribution lines of the private power companies, and hoped for favorable purchase prices. In five cases the jury award as to the value of the electric lines was rejected as being too high. Whatcom PUD on August 7, 1940, received an award of $5 million; Lewis PUD on May 10, 1942, for $2.1 million; Cowlitz PUD $1.1 million on May 10, 1942; Thurston PUD $4.4 million on May 10, 1942; and Snohomish PUD $9.9 million March 19, 1943. In retrospect, the awards were reasonable and the PUDs soon realized that they should have gone ahead. As a result both Thurston and Whatcom gave up on acquiring the Puget Sound Power and Light Company lines in their respective counties. The other three did acquire later at higher prices.

The acquisition process was muddied by a divisive debate as to whether acquisitions should be made by negotiation, mainly by financier Guy Myers, or by condemnation suits. Another debate was between acquiring the PSP&L system as a unit, generation and all, versus the county by county approach.

But a futile decade of effort resulted in no acquisition of any major company's entire system. The approach was flawed and subject to endless delays which favored the private utilities. Meanwhile, the availability of low-cost BPA power enabled the private utilities to become financially strong and better able to resist takeover by the PUDs.

In 13 cases PUDs did take over via condemnation those portions of private utility electric distribution lines located in their respective counties: Clallam, 1944, of PSP&L; Cowlitz, 1940, of Washington Gas & Electric, and in 1946 of Northwestern Electric. Douglas, Grant and Okanogan in 1945 acquired Washington Water Power; Skamania in 1942 took over Northwestern Electric and Pacific Power & Light; Benton in 1946, PP&L; Franklin 1947, PP&L; Clark in 1946, Portland General Electric, and in 1948, PP&L; and Klickitat, 1947, PP&L. In 22 cases PUDs negotiated their acquisitions. Because of the many small companies involved, some PUDs had to make two or more acquisitions.

The private utilities opposed public power in county after county, year after year as illustrated by Clark County PUD. It was formed in 1938 and went into business August 22, 1942, serving Vancouver Shipyard and several large housing projects by underbidding the two private utilities. A "sleeper" candidate, Elmer Deetz became commissioner and opposed taking over private utilities.

Sleeper candidates were regularly elected in some counties and they often succeeded in putting their PUDs "to sleep." The other two commissioners condemned and took over Portland General Electric Company lines in 1946. An avowed opponent to acquisition of private utilities filed against Commissioner Heye H. Meyer, one of the originators of the PUD. Meyer, a Granger, won easily in 1946. In 1948, the other private utility lines, those owned by PP&L, were condemned and acquired.

Banner PUD years were 1948 when 50,000 customers were taken over from the private utilities, and 1949 when Snohomish PUD went into business with 38,000 customers. By 1952 the acquisition process was essentially complete, and the 22 PUDs were then serving 197,607 electric customers or 23 percent of Washington's population.

Berry Writes About PUDs. Also in 1952, on December 19, Editor Ted Berry published a 16-page *Grange News* on The PUD Story. He did the Grange proud.

Berry (1903-1973) was an honor graduate of the University of Washington School of Journalism, working for several papers before becoming editor of *The Grange News* in 1935.

When he died in 1973, he had been editor 38 years. The PUDs were his favorite subject. In 1940, he married Rose Anita Slavin of a prominent Grange family in Yakima. They had three children. He was a farm leader in helping farmers through his editorials and writing. He was an excellent photographer and musician. He wrote the Washington State Grange song. The Grange Leadership Award was given to him in 1972. Anita Berry joined *The Grange News* in 1957 as circulation manager, and in 1975 became secretary to the state master, and later also office manager, retiring in 1987.

Legislative Leadership. During the Carstensen period the main legislative issues concerned public power. Initiative 12 was enacted by the Legislature in 1943 to enable two or more PUDs to act jointly to acquire power facilities.

Private utilities succeeded in putting it on the ballot as Referendum 25 and defeated it. Thus emboldened, the private utilities put Initiative 166 on the ballot to require a vote of the people on all PUD revenue bonds. The people in 1946 voted it down. The two votes illustrate the stalemate that existed. The PUDs could not get an easy way to acquire an entire large private utility. The private utilities could not force a vote on each PUD bond issue.

Outstanding among the many Grangers who have served in the Washington Legislature has been Charles William Hodde. Born in Missouri in 1906, he graduated from high school there before moving to a rented potato farm near Colville in Stevens County in 1930, joined the Grange and passed out literature favoring the 1930 PUD initiative. In 1933, Hodde married Helen Lolo Mighell. They had three children. He purchased his farm in 1937.

He became master of Fort Colville Grange and attended the 1931 State Grange session in Bellingham. Goss asked Hodde to campaign for the 40 mill limit on property tax, to seek enactment of a state income tax and to serve as Grange representative during legislative sessions. The 40 mill tax limit and the income tax were passed, but the Supreme Court declared the income tax unconstitutional. Hodde served as State Grange lecturer 1933 to 1937. In 1935, he lobbied the blanket primary initiative through the Legislature. He was State Grange overseer 1953-1957 and again 1971-1972.

He served in the State House of Representatives 1937-38 and again between 1943 and 1952, the last four years as speaker. Few fields of legislation have missed his touch, but mainly he was regarded as an authority on taxes and finance, as a public power supporter, a friend of better education for rural areas, good roads and forestry. After failing in his try for the governorship in 1952, he served on numerous state commissions and in administrative capacities both federal and state. In 1962, he received the State Grange Leadership Award. A book of Hodde jokes would be a best seller.

Chemurgy Chimera. A new word burst upon the farm scene in the late 1930s and faded away almost as fast in less than two decades. "Chemurgy" the dictionaries generalized as "chemistry at work." The specific definition was "the branch of chemistry dealing with the use of farm products in the manufacture of new products other than food or clothing." An example is soybeans as a base for plastics.

Kegley around 1910 became an enthusiast for use of farm wastes to produce alcohol. That idea was revived in 1942 and again in the late 1970s when the U.S. built alcohol plants. In the late 1930s the National Farm Chemurgic Council was formed. It held annual conferences to describe and show how farm waste and surplus crops could be turned into profitable products. Owners of patents sought sponsors for financing processing plants. War prices helped to create a climate of optimism.

Ervin King in 1937 referred to "New Uses" such as alcohol but cautioned that they must be competitive. His last four Master's Addresses (1938-1941) used the "Chemurgy" subhead and he thought it would be of growing importance. Starting in 1941 the Chemurgy Committee appeared as a special Grange committee.

Carstensen in 1942 cited the soybean industry in the Middle West and growing paper pulp in Texas as chemurgy. In 1943, Carstensen announced that war shortages provided the opportunity the Grange had sought. Northwest Chemurgy Cooperative had been established and equipment was purchased to produce glucose at Wenatchee. He made, however, some telling comments, that no financial assistance was available from any governmental source, and that revenue from the first plant would help in establishing additional plants. He added that with minor modifications the Wenatchee plant could produce any of some 62 products depending on the market. And he predicted such plants would be part of a permanent industry after the war. Financing was done by farmers purchasing stock and pledging commodities for processing. In 1944,

Carstensen reported the Wenatchee plant producing starch and glucose from excess potatoes and wheat. Manager Ronald Smith of Northwest Chemurgy Cooperative in 1944 reported acquiring a potato starch-glucose plant at Lynden and start of construction of a potato starch plant at Ellensburg.

In 1946, optimism still prevailed on the future of chemurgy. Carstensen's1947 report cited net profit of $166,000 for the Wenatchee and Ellensburg plants. However, financial difficulties had arisen in the expansion program at Tulelake, California, Klamath Falls and The Dalles, Oregon. The future nonetheless appeared bright, he said.

Carstensen reported in 1948 that the end of sugar rationing had upset the glucose market forcing Northwest Chemurgy Cooperative into bankruptcy. An intermediate cause was the cancellation of a contract by Orange Crush. He hoped things would be squared away so the Wenatchee plant could resume operations. Because of delays, the same hopes were expressed in 1949 but that year Washington agriculture slumped. Carstensen's brief eight and one-half page 1950 Master's Address did not mention chemurgy. The Chemurgy Committee urged more funding for Washington State University and University of Washington for study of chemurgy possibilities. However, the Chemurgy Committee was no longer a special com-

Each summer, hundreds of children attend one of several camps sponsored by the State Grange junior department.

mittee and after 1950 the word chemurgy was no longer mentioned in the Proceedings. Carstensen personally invested in chemurgy and led many others to invest. Many lost all of their investment. Some farmers who were able to sell surplus potatoes and wheat gained a little. Mainly the chemurgy venture appeared unbusinesslike, and "overoptimistic." At the 1950 annual session the Grievances Committee deplored the attempts of one Edwin S. Parker to attack the executive committee and the master, and recommmended that Parker be censured. The Everett session of the State Grange in 1950 adopted this recommendation.

Youth Camp. The employment of a full-time Juvenile matron in 1944 had resulted by 1953 in doubling the number of Juvenile Granges. Also in 1944, the Grange executive committee began planning the Ervin E. King Memorial Recreation Park and began looking for a centrally located site.

The 1948 Master's Address announced jubilantly that the site had been found on the Sunset Highway at Lake Kachess just east of Snoqualmie Pass. The executive committee first took an option on the 32.5 acre Rustic Inn property, raised the $28,000 by subscriptions and completed the purchase by creating the Grange Recreation and Education Association with Richard G. Hedges as president.

By 1950, Rustic Inn was used by a small group of campers and by 1952 had 1,000 attending in the course of the summer. In his last Master's Address Carstensen predicted "The future success of the youth camp appears certain..." Well, there were problems. The State Highway Department built a limited access highway that did not help Rustic Inn. Getting electricity was difficult. The brief summer use by Grange youngsters could not support the investment. It required year around commercial use and caretaker management. However, that led to many problems and deficits. Also, some Grange families felt Rustic Inn was too far away. The deficits continued for two more years.

The Carstensen era brought a 30 percent surge in Grange membership, pushing the total over the 50,000 mark. GIA added the third floor to the Grange headquarters, moving in during July 1949. National Master Goss died in 1950.

Budget restraints started with the agricultural downturn in 1949 and resulted in changing the juvenile matron to part-time, and in reduction in staff and deputies.

Despite minor problems, the Washington State Grange became stronger and better as a result of Carstensen's dedication and energetic leadership.

CHAPTER ELEVEN

NELSON: 1953 - 1971

IN THE PUBLIC INTEREST

"There is a tide in the affairs of men,
Which, taken at the flood, leads on to fortune;
Omitted, all the voyage of their life
Is bound in shallows and in miseries."

"Julius Caesar"
William Shakespeare

Lars Nelson picked a good time to be state master. If he could do it over again, he would likely choose the same 18 years from 1953 to 1971. The country was rebuilding. It was a time of fairly steady, postwar growth. Agriculture expanded its horizons with mechanization, chemicals and fertilizers. The tide was usually favorable.

The Grange expanded its programs in agriculture, the interstate highway system, major new electric power developments and other public concerns. Grange membership increased by 10,000.

A. Lars Nelson (1909-1971) was the tenth master of the Washington State Grange. He was elected in June 1953 and served over 18 years, a period longer than any other Washington State Grange master.

He was born April 16, 1909, on a wheat farm between St. John and Thornton in Whitman County. After graduating in 1931 from Willamette University, he did graduate studies both at Washington State College and, while teaching political science, at Syracuse University. He joined Wheatland Grange No. 952 in 1933 because, "During the depression it was the only organization helping the farmer economically, socially...to help agriculture get a square deal." In 1935, he married Rose Wetherell of Baker, Oregon. She was graduated from Willamette University with honors, did graduate studies at the University of Wisconsin and taught school. They had two children, a son and a daughter. Rose was Washington State Mother of the Year in 1960, and was highly regarded in the Grange. She died in 1965.

In 1937, Nelson took over the family farm and diversified it by growing wheat, other grains, hay, shorthorn cattle and Chester White hogs. He served as master of Wheatland Grange and as Whitman County Pomona master, belonged to more than 20 other organizations, committees and commissions, and was National

A. Lars Nelson

Grange overseer 10 years. In 1967 he married Olga Wilson, former secretary to the Oregon State Grange master and editor of the *Oregon Grange Bulletin* and then of the *Northwest Public Power Bulletin*. He died in office October 9, 1971.

Early Hurdles. The uneasy circumstances which led to Nelson's election did not disappear. Chemurgy, of course, had ended as a Grange effort several years before the election. The Rustic Inn problem continued.

Nelson brought at least one problem of his own. He had not been involved in the Grange program of electric power development and people did not know his views on power. Before the end of 1953, the Eisenhower administration provided a real challenge for Nelson as a Republican.

The Republican Congress and the Eisenhower administration took turns in bashing public power. The Truman budget was junked and replaced with a private power mandate to curtail federal power budgets and to circumvent the power marketing preference clause. Bonneville Power Administration was ordered to stop construction of a major 230,000 volt transmission line to Klamath Falls and sell out its right of way and material to a private utility. The line was to have been a step toward an intertie with California and was considered of strategic importance.

Secretary of the Interior Douglas McKay ordered BPA to give 20-year firm power contracts to the private utilities. He canceled the Bureau of Reclamation plans to build the high Hells Canyon Dam on the Snake River and paved the way for the Idaho Power Company to build three small power dams instead with virtually no flood control storage or downstream power benefits. Interior's Undersecretary Ralph Tudor and Assistant Secretary Fred Aandahl made speeches charging that public power was attempting to nationalize electric utilities and put the country on the road to socialism.

Nelson didn't take long to make clear that he was a Theodore Roosevelt advocate of the wise use of natural resources. Nelson favored full development of the Hells Canyon damsite, the public power and rural electrification programs, and he deplored the so-called Eisenhower partnership program. In a November 1953 speech he took his stand with the Washington PUD Association and brought his audience to its feet. He became a firm public power leader.

There need have been no doubt where Lars Nelson stood. His mother, a woman with a strong will, had no use for the Washington Water Power Company. She strongly supported Inland Power and Light Company, an REA borrower cooperative, which served the Nelson farm. Nelson knew the three Grangers who formed Inland: Dan Hopkins, Leo Thams and E. Arnold Burgess.

In 1954, Nelson reported that the Grange was hard pressed financially because of the $15,000 of Rustic Inn costs. He estimated deficits of $20,000 per year for at least five years. The bleak report led delegates to vote for selling Rustic Inn. While the sales effort was underway several prominent Grangers including Charles F. Keiser, Fred Berger and Naomi Tolonen offered to buy the camp. They adopted the name Washington Youth Activities, Inc. WYA proposed to continue to operate as a camp usable by Grange youngsters, the selling price was lowered to $75,000, and the transaction was completed as of June 1, 1955.

In 1956, WYA failed to meet its payments to the Grange but felt it could refinance if the price was reduced a further $15,000. The Grange agreed and the sale was completed. Thereupon the Grange Recreation and Education Association was dissolved. The building of a non-access highway through the Rustic Inn property put WYA out of business in 1958. WYA donated the residual $6,000 to Washington State University. Interest earned on the money has supported the Ervin E. King Memorial Scholarship for a junior or senior boy or girl majoring in agriculture or home economics respectively. The WYA was dissolved in 1963.

Meanwhile, the juvenile and youth departments of the Grange had selected five decentralized camps, including Rustic Inn. These operated on a trial basis in 1955, were well received and set the pattern for the future. Ted and Lena Lloyd were leaders for many years.

Scale of Operations. Nelson was a large man with a booming voice, and his scale of operation seemed to follow one rule—bigger.

The membership increase of almost 20 percent in 18 years under Nelson was one of slow, steady gain. The early years were handicapped because of old controversies. Membership had fallen from 50,894 at the end of 1953 to 48,667 at the end of 1957. Two surges of growth came from 1957 to 1962 with a gain of 5,401 Grangers, and from 1963 to 1971 a gain of 6,541, closing 1971 at 60,363. The latter gain occurred while GIA auto insurance was a real bargain.

Membership turnover led Nelson to urge statewide efforts to retain existing members. His analysis showed a loss of 8.37 and gain of 8.46 members per Grange in 1964. The totals were 4,011 added and 3,968 dropped including 714 deaths. He also noted that the U.S. average age was 29 but Grange members averaged over 50, hence he urged focus on young people. For many years Washington stood fourth in members among Grange states, following Ohio, New York and Pennsylvania. His last address showed only Ohio ahead.

Some indicators of the larger scale of operations appear in the published Proceedings of the annual sessions. Carstensen averaged 200 pages. Nelson began at 285 pages in 1954 and set an all time record of 463 pages in 1971. His last Master's Address alone required 153 pages.

Come to the Fair! A big responsibility of the Grange is to promote Grange participation in the fairs.

Come August and September, Grangers find their feet taking them to the fair. They hear the song:

"The sun is ashining to welcome the day,
Heigh-ho! come to the fair!
The folk are all singing so merry and gay,
Heigh-ho! come to the fair!"

—Helen Taylor

The fair is like a powerful magnet because Grangers of all ages are involved. Many Grange families get ready for the fair all year.

Thousands of blue, red and white ribbons and other prizes and

Colorful Grange booths at Washington's fairs always attract crowds. The chief purpose of the booths is to educate consumers about the diversity and importance of agriculture in the state.

recognition are handed out by the judges for every breed of livestock, horses, cattle, sheep, pigs, goats, poultry, rabbits, pigeons, flowers, fresh and canned produce, sewing, handicrafts, art and much more.

Most fairs have a Grange building where each local Grange has an exhibit in competition. Often these exhibits feature the quality and diversity of fruits, vegetables and other agricultural produce. The cornucopia is often the main symbol. It is the horn of plenty, overflowing with fruits,vegetables, grains and flowers.

Fairs have existed since time immemorial. The market or commercial fairs in both the Orient and the West predate history. Marco Polo reported on the great fairs of China. The Aztecs of Mexico had fairs.

The word comes from the Latin *feria,* a holiday or feast day. Long before the Romans, fairs were a means of carrying on peaceful trade. Even when at war, the opponents would meet on the fairgrounds under a truce.

France records the fairs at Champagne and Brie in the year 427. After the Norman Conquest, fairs became common in England.

In the United States, the focus has been on agricultural education through the exhibition of produce and handicrafts. City and country people came together at the fair. Many city people know of the Grange by visiting the fair.

Washington fairs stand high among the states. In 1985, of the 50 top fairs in the U.S. the Ohio State Fair, a 16-day run, led all others with an attendance of 3.6 million. In eleventh place was the Western Washington Fair at Puyallup with 1,234,278, also 16 days. The Oregon State Fair was 23rd with 756,576 attendance, the 10-day Evergreen State Fair at Monroe was 29th at 666,000 and the eight-day Clark County Fair stood as number 31 at 634,708.

The Washington State Fair Association lists 71 fairs annually ranging from the livestock fairs of April, May and June and the county and larger fairs of July, August and September. Smaller fairs are usually two to four days.

Fairs usually comprise four elements: agricultural exhibits and judging; commercial exhibits; entertainment; and food. The fairs are big business!

Farm to Market Roads. Decade by decade the Grange exerted its influence and has worked with other groups to promote good roads for Washington.

Initially the Grangers called for local control of road building at the county level, and many Grangers hitched their horses to wagons, scrapers and the Fresno shovel to do road building and maintenance. Heavy forests, steep mountain slopes and swampy lands complicated the building of Washington roads. The Indians had traveled by canoe on the waters of Puget Sound and the Columbia River system or followed centuries-old trails, many worn 18 inches deep. The early explorers and fur traders followed the Indian water routes and land trails. In 1853, the Oregon Legislature let a contract for a wagon road up the east bank of the Cowlitz River to connect with trails leading to Puget Sound.

Citizens around Puget Sound, expecting an emigrant train, launched a wagon road in 1853 across Naches Pass. They made little progress. That fall the emigrant train arrived and had to winch their wagons down a thousand foot drop at 45 degrees. It took a month for them to reach Parkland. Animals and pack loads went by switchback trail.

General George B. McClellan, then a captain, was in charge of building the Naches Pass road in 1854.

The new Legislature of Washington Territory in 1854 proceeded to identify future wagon roads by widening the Indian trails. Generally these radiated out from Steilacoom to reach Bellingham,

Seattle, Grays Harbor, Cathlamet and Vancouver. These were the roads described as the "Pioneer Roads" in an excellent article in the first issue (October 1, 1912) of the *Agricultural Grange News*. It was read at the Woman's Good Road Congress in Tacoma.

The Good Roads movement sprang up in Washington State around 1900. An early leader was Sam Hill, general counsel of the Great Northern Railroad. Grangers suspected Sam Hill of favoring mainly short roads to feed traffic to the GN. The farmers wanted farm-to-market roads. Often they referred to roads proposed by city people as pleasuring roads for Sunday drivers.

The 1853-1889 territorial period saw very little road building; there was little money. The military wagon roads, such as the Mullan Road from Walla Walla to Fort Benton, Montana, were, however, built in this period.

After achieving statehood, Washington lost no time in establishing a department of highways. Progress was slow because of the scarcity of money. The advent of the automobile, trucks and rural free delivery of mail helped Grangers in promoting their farm-to-market roads. Nonetheless, the diaries, letters and newspapers reported that the roads either produced billowing and choking dust or let the wheels become mired in mud.

Grangers became weary from talking about it. Paradoxically, the subject on which Grangers worked so hard at all levels and in all counties was barely mentioned in State Grange Proceedings. Perhaps the reason is that many Grangers became county commissioners or members of the Legislature where they could do something about building and improving roads. In the mid-1950s as the interstate highway system was announced, the Washington State Grange gave its support.

The state of Washington has 42,000 miles of paved roads and highways at all levels of government. The Grange has been involved. The Department of Transportation (DOT) also includes emergency airports and the ferry system. DOT reports that 58 percent of Washington traffic is on 7,000 miles of interstate and state highways.

Agricultural Economist. Nelson usually gave two addresses. He covered the internal business of the Grange under "Good of the Order." The much larger effort was the "Agriculture's Economic Position," in which he digested his reading of the year. He was foremost an agricultural economist reporting on developments, trends and the changing structure of agriculture.

He was a prolific writer and a good writer. He could often be seen with a legal size yellow pad so he could write whether at the head table during a banquet, or seated in the audience, in a hotel lobby, or while traveling. Always he was picking up ideas and better ways of expressing thoughts. His Master's Addresses became the final depositories of each year's dredging for golden prose: An example, in a discussion of booster night—"The fire of purpose, sacrifice and endeavor must be rekindled." He made extensive use of statistics and reproduced charts and graphs in his Master's Address. But he did not stop with farming issues. Much of his address reported on electric power, highways, taxes, prices, income and other public interest areas.

Grange speakers found many ideas in Nelson's vast compilations. Certainly his analysis and point of view became respected in Olympia and at the National Grange. His Master's Address contained the evidence and logic for his recommendations to the Grange delegates.

Nelson had the State Grange system of committees very much in mind as he wrote the Master's Address. He would address the area of responsibility of each committee as a way of reaffirming his belief that each committee was still needed. The process also resulted in committee changes. Thus the Master's Address served to integrate the combined assignments of the committees.

The Structure of Agriculture. The Master's Addresses became a textbook of agricultural economics, organized by years from 1954 through 1971. Nelson organized his subjects under three perspectives: the national picture, the state picture and the picture of each major agricultural commodity produced in Washington. This was his basic structure.

Nationally he dwelt on the inexorable annual drop in farm population and the increased size of farms. He traced the decline in prices and their tendency to trail far below parity. His graphs showed the cost-price squeeze as production costs rose and crop prices declined. He regularly reported on the rising productivity and efficiency of agriculture.

At the state level he reported the increased number of farms and then the turnaround and annual decline in the number of farms. He reported total farm income and farm acreage. Some years brought sharp drops in income.

Nelson was most in his element in discussing individual farm commodities. Every year he listed the income of Washington farmers from each commodity, usually the top 15 crops or products.

For many years he studied laws of other states establishing commissions to promote individual farm commodities. In 1955 and 1961 the Grange obtained enabling legislation in Washington. His 1956

Master's Address devoted three pages to the method of establishing a commission through referendum of the growers of that crop; the role of the commission in promoting the use and sale of that commodity; research; standards and other concerns; and a tax within each group to pay the costs. The state director of agriculture supervises the commissions and the marketing order applicable to each. The legislation authorizing the commodity commissions may prove to be the chief legacy of the Nelson era.

Public Power Makes Strides. Nelson in 1953 found himself catapulted into the controversy over the Eisenhower partnership policy. He landed on his feet and was soon fighting on the side of public power.

He took a ringside seat by accepting appointments on power advisory boards including the Bonneville Power Regional Advisory Board, Western States Water and Power Consumers Conference, the Washington State Power Users, and the Utilities and Transportation Advisory Council to the Utilities and Transportation Commission. The Grange was a charter member of the National Hells Canyon Association and contributed $1,000 per year for at least six years.

The power partnership policy was hard on the Pacific Northwest in 1953 and 1954, but softened appreciably when the Republicans lost their House and Senate majorities in November 1954. The election of Senator Richard L. Neuberger of Oregon was the one-vote switch which changed the Senate. Neuberger had attacked the partnership policy as a front for private power. The 1956 election was decisive in the Northwest in killing partnership. The chief loss was the high Hells Canyon Dam.

Washington's militant Senators Warren G. Magnuson and Henry M. Jackson together with friendly, conservation-minded senators from Oregon, Idaho, Montana and other Western states kept the federal power program going. Nelson worked closely with the Congress.

The capacity of the Bonneville Power system doubled from 1953 to 1961. Rural electrification reached about 99 percent of the farmers in the Pacific Northwest by 1960. The Washington State Grange adopted innumerable resolutions on public power.

With the coming of the Kennedy administration and the appointment of Charles F. Luce of Walla Walla as BPA administrator, the region became a beehive of power activity. In the brief span of five years from 1961 to 1966 the Congress had approved the Canadian Treaty, the West Coast Interties, Grand Coulee Third Powerplant, Hanford Generating Plant and was pouring $100 million yearly into

Sen. Henry M. Jackson, center, was one of the dignitaries who became a regular guest at annual State Grange conventions. He is seen here visiting with State Master A. Lars Nelson, right, and Horace Bozarth, executive committeeman, during the 1968 session.

transmission line construction. Senator Jackson called this period the golden age for hydro.

Behind these headline-grabbing federal activities, the Washington PUDs were quietly coming into their own, expanding service and reducing rates. They had gone through the Goss era, which passed the PUD initiative of 1930, the King era of PUD formation, the Carstensen era of getting into business, and now under Nelson came the fourth season, that of the harvest. The 22 PUDs operating electric systems at the end of 1952 were serving 197,607 customers, or 23 percent of the Washington population, and were selling electricity for home use at 1.25 cents per kwh, a rate only a half to a fourth of the rates in existence before World War II. In 1970, they served 336,417 customers at an average residential rate of only 0.87 cents per kwh. The PUDs were in excellent financial condition.

Chelan PUD acquired the Chelan Falls Powerhouse, acquired and expanded the Rock Island Dam, and built the Rocky Reach Dam. Grant PUD built Wanapum and Priest Rapids dams. Douglas PUD built Wells Dam. Pend Oreille PUD built the Box Canyon Dam. PUDs harnessed hydro which, it appeared, would not qualify as federal projects. For $1.5 billion the PUDs had more than four million kilowatts of generating capacity.

A group of 17 Washington cities and PUDs in 1957, after a decade of legislative effort, formed the Washington Public Power Supply System, which built the 860,000 kw Hanford generating plant 1962 to 1966. It utilized the energy of steam from the new production reactor which otherwise would have gone wasted. Senator Jackson and President Kennedy hailed it as a dual purpose project. Kennedy's ground breaking speech said it was a way of beating atomic swords into plowshares. As the 1960 decade drew to a close, WPPSS was getting ready to build three nuclear plants, Washington Nuclear Plant No. 1 and No. 2 at Hanford and WNP No. 3 at Satsop. Thus the Nelson era witnessed the region's shift from hydro to interties and was launching the hydro thermal power program with emphasis on nuclear power and coal-fired generation. The Grange half-century battle for the PUDs had paid off.

In 1958, the author, as executive secretary of the Northwest Public Power Association, was privileged to address the Washington State Grange annual session on "The Miracle River of America," advocating more upstream storage on the Columbia River tributaries. A more frequent participant at annual sessions was Ken Billington of the Washington PUD Association, also a Granger.

Pursuing the Public Interest. By 1910, Washington State Grange Master Kegley recognized that farmers were no longer in the majority. He made alliances with labor and other minority groups to pursue common legislative goals. Grangers learned the wisdom of advocating and voting for proposals that reached beyond the normal concern of farmers.

As Grange representatives in Olympia succeeded in helping to pass the initiative and referendum package, direct election of senators, woman suffrage, the direct and blanket primaries, the PUD law and others, it became apparent that Grange success depended on the public interest breadth of the proposal. Whenever the Grange advocated something that had application to the public at large and not just to Grangers, it was more likely to be passed.

Perennial legislative subjects that remained on the Grange agenda included the Torrens system of recording land titles. This

Australian method, used in a number of countries and states, virtually eliminated the need for title insurance. Legislative redistricting and reapportionment of congressional districts regularly received Grange attention. The oldest subject introduced by the first territorial Legislature was that of roads and highways. Schools, taxes, cost of government, game, forests, safety, insurance, crime, pesticides and interest rates were among the many legislative subjects which affected Grangers just as much as they did the average citizen. Thus the Grange was not going out of its place in taking on such broad public interest concerns.

In representing the Grange during the legislative session Nelson was never alone. He had a legislative team that varied in size and he had many friends in both chambers, within the state offices and alliances among organizations. Russ Holt, then on Senator Jackson's staff, recalls that the senator admired Nelson and regarded his advice as trustworthy. By coincidence, Horace William Bozarth (1894-1976) of Douglas County was on the House Agricultural Committee and for many years as chairman (1954 to 1972). He had supported the Grange power bill in 1930, was a charter member of Delrio Grange No. 828 and its first master for 12 years, Pomona master 25 years. A 50-year Granger, Bozarth regretted that he once missed attending the Grange annual session. He received the Grange Leadership Award in 1960.

Bozarth may have launched the surprise House resolution paying tribute to Lars Nelson. Nelson was seated in the gallery when the House members gave him a standing ovation.

CHAPTER TWELVE

SILVERS: 1971 - 1983

WINNING THE FAMILY FARM WATER STRUGGLE

"...all the great values of this (Western) territory have ultimately to be measured to you in acre-feet."
John Wesley Powell

Jack Silvers was born thirsty for water, and he soon learned to fear corporate monopoly over water. He was impressed by the above words used by John Wesley Powell in addressing the Montana Constitutional Convention in Helena in 1889. They applied equally to North Dakota, South Dakota and Washington, which became states in 1889 and to Idaho and Wyoming upon statehood in 1890. Silvers was aware that Powell had studied the relationship of water and land in the Western states for two decades before concluding that full use of available water could irrigate only 12 percent of the land. In 1878, Powell handed Secretary of the Interior Carl Schurz his report on the arid lands, which called for dams to capture and store the flood waters and release them as needed for irrigation. Silvers held with Wallace Stegner, who, in his life of Powell summarizes a view not easily grasped by people from the humid Eastern states: "Water is the true wealth in a dry land. Without it, land is worthless or nearly so, and if you control the water, you control the land that depends on it. In that fact alone was the ominous threat of land and water monopolies."

Jack Silvers was born in Yakima September 27, 1922, grew up on a 42-acre fruit ranch, majored in agriculture at Washington State University, and launched his own 32-acre orchard north of Zillah in 1944.

The many Grange programs, activities and legislative efforts could easily overshadow the important Grange role in leadership training. The ritual observed at meetings helps the new Granger to begin training in minor roles and become accustomed to performing in public. The minor roles and rituals evolve into positions of increasing responsibility. Officers thus may come up through the ranks in a genuine democratic process. In the case of Jack Silvers the leadership training involved many ranks and many years of apprenticeship.

He served as a junior Grange master in 1934, joined Buena Grange No. 836 in 1944, served as master 1947-1949, Pomona master 1951-1953, deputy master 17 years, state assistant steward 1949-1955, state steward 1955-1957, state overseer 1957-1971, organized five Granges, served as state master 1971-1983, and as a member of the state executive committee since 1983. For six years, 1969-1975, Silvers served as chairman of the Washington Highway Users Federation, and continued on the board of directors four more years. In 1983, he was on the executive committee of the Washington State Good Roads and Transportation Association. He served on numerous committees including first chairman of the State Grange Historical Committee. He became a member of the National Grange executive committee in 1976 and has served as secretary and chairman of the committee.

During his 14 years as state overseer, he spent about a month each year assisting in compiling and organizing Nelson's massive Master's Addresses. Thus he gained a special background in the many issues of concern to farmers.

Family Farm Threatened. Silvers took office at a time when, in just 18 years, the number of farms in the U.S. had been cut in half.

Jack Silvers

Initiative 59 coordinators for the State Grange watched Bruce Bishop of the Washington State Labor Council sign the initiative during a meeting at Grange headquarters in 1976. From the left are Homer Trefry, Paul Holmes, Ray Hill, Brian Royer (a consultant working with the committee), Bishop, Ray Schneider, Les Snyder and Fred Yahn.

As Nelson told Grangers, three million farms disappeared, leaving three million. Generally, the loss amounted to 3 percent per year with some years twice that percentage of loss. In his early years as master, Nelson reported very few corporate farms, by which he meant corporations other than family farm corporations. But by 1969 he was troubled by the rapid trend toward fewer and larger farms. So was Silvers.

Silvers' first Master's Address in 1972 took a swipe at "Tax Loss Farming" whereby farm development costs were written off against nonfarm profits. In time Congress limited this to $25,000 per year, but the entire concept of tax loss farming was contrary to the longstanding congressional policy to preserve the family farm.

In 1973, Silvers said, "The Washington State Grange actively supports the concept of the family farm as a basic unit of production in American agriculture. We have endorsed the raising of the basic irrigation limitation to 160 acres, recognizing that changes in farming techniques require more acreage to achieve an economy of scale. But to remove the acreage limitation entirely, would be to condone the already accelerating movement of American agriculture into large commercial holdings. Therefore, in view of our continuing support for the family farm concept, we oppose complete lifting of the acreage limitation, as suggested in the (National Water Commission) draft report." Also in 1973, Grangers adopted a resolution calling on the Legislature to discourage the encroachment of conglomerate corporations into the farming field in Washington. The resolution asked that if the Legislature did not enact the bill, an initiative be presented for a vote of the people.

By 1974, however, Silvers reported that surveys indicated that the issue of conglomerate corporations versus the family farm was not well understood by the public and was not ready for the initiative route.

The 1975 Master's Address devoted four pages to summarize a report "Income Tax Rules and Agriculture" resulting from a seminar featuring 10 speakers at the University of Missouri-Columbia in December 1974. The theme was that the tax laws and rules favor big scale farming. Speaker after speaker called for corrective action to preserve the family farm and ranch concept.

Washington state farm income passed the $2 billion mark in 1975 only three years after passing the $1 billion level in 1972. Record crops, rampant inflation, good markets and the bounty of the Columbia Basin Project were among the factors. But things were not as good for the farmer as that might seem. Unfortunately, inflation increased costs even more for farming machinery, fertilizer, seed, fuel and chemicals.

In 1976, Silvers used the Master's Address to lay a foundation for action. On "Conglomerate Corporate Farming" he quoted from the November 1975 issue of "Catholic Rural Life" and a 1971 U.S. Senate report on monopoly, which contrasted the rural life of two Central Valley towns of California. The town surrounded by small farms enjoyed a richer community life and a greater sum of those values for which America stands, as compared with the large-farm town surrounded by a few industrialized farms. Silvers feared what industrialized farming would do to rural life in Washington.

Next there followed five pages summarizing "Corporate Farming Statutes" of 10 states which limited or prohibited farming by corporations.

"Tax Loss Farming" was his next subject, summarizing a bulletin of the Economic Research Service of the U.S. Department of Agriculture. It concluded that tax loss farming was affecting the economics of agriculture and Silvers concluded that reforms were needed.

He then turned to the "Horse Heaven Development" where one application had been made for a permit for sufficient water for farming 100,000 acres. Silvers suggested that there was a question as to whether this type of development would be in the best interest of the public and the state of Washington. Then he summarized the evolution of the laws on water rights in Washington.

The 1976 State Grange convention delegates voted to direct the executive committee to prepare and circulate a petition putting before the Legislature an initiative to control the trend toward corporate farming by restricting irrigation water allocations above that reasonably necessary for a family size farm operation.

The 1977 Master's Address devoted six pages to Initiative No. 59, the Family Farm Water Act. Chief draftsman of the Act was Charlie Hodde, former speaker of the Washington House of Representatives and veteran of many legislative wars. First he was meticulously careful to protect all existing water rights, and indeed allowed the holder of existing water rights to apply for an additional water right for an acreage qualifying as a family farm.

Second, Hodde drafted the act to allow a developer a period of 10 to 20 years to develop and subdivide larger acreage into units that would qualify as family farms.

The family farm was defined by the act as not including more than 2,000 acres of irrigated agricultural land per person in the family and not counting dry land holdings. It also provided that a family farm could be leased. All of these provisions were designed to show that the act leaned over backwards in an effort to be fair to any moderate size farm enterprise including bona fide family farm corporations.

Enacting the Family Farm Water Act. In a four month period the Grange and a dozen supporting organizations collected over 192,000 signatures. Only 123,711 were needed to validate the initiative to the Legislature. More than 300 people became members of the century club by obtaining 100 or more signups. Virtually every county reached the goal set up before the start of the campaign.

These were the chief arguments used in the campaign as explained in the 1977 Master's Address: "The Grange believes strongly that the best assurance of a dependable food supply is maintenance and support of the family farm. The Grange is not talking of family farming in the sense of small uneconomic units largely dependent on family labor. Today's family farm is an efficient, well equipped, scientific business. It, nevertheless, retains that important element of pride of ownership of the land and sense of responsibility to the community necessary to stability of food production and support of the nonbusiness amenities of our state. There are several ways in which large expansion into agricultural irrigated farming by corporate business, especially food processing conglomerates, threatens the viability of family farming and the benefits to the community of family farmers as a base.

"Large scale farming by corporations gives that corporation, which may also process agricultural products, an undue advantage in bargaining with independent farmers for prices of the crops they process and threatens the present producers with a certain loss of much of their market.

"Huge corporate farming developments will not be accompanied by development of balanced communities of property owning citizens contributing to the support of basic elements of a good life and the support of local business. Employment being largely seasonal they more likely will cause severe social problems for surrounding communities that must absorb the seasonally unemployed.

"Corporate developers with significant taxable income outside their farming enterprises are getting a very substantial federal subsidy through investment credits, accelerated depreciation of improvements, tax loss writeoffs against other income, and other cost savings through concentration of their farming operations in low population density areas with low property tax rates as well as benefiting through greater bargaining power in both purchasing and marketing.

"Operating through subsidiary corporations, the parent corporation can collect the profits while enjoying protection from unusual liability if some part of their farming ventures prove unprofitable. If a project becomes more profitable as a tax write-off than as a farm operation, they can abandon it and leave any residual problems for the surrounding communities to absorb."

The Legislature did not enact the initiative, hence it went on the general election ballot. Governor Evans offered staff assistance. Governor Dixy Lee Ray supported the initiative both in her campaign and in her inaugural address.

The November 8, 1977, election was close. Initiative 59 was close in the major urban areas but won in rural areas. It carried in 29 of the 39 counties and went into the statutes as the Family Farm Water Act.

Membership Reaches Peak. Grangers in Washington set a new peak of 54,825 members in 1948 under Carstensen, then sagged to 48,667 by 1957 and passed the Carstensen peak in 1967. Thus the 1948 to 1967 period was a 20-year plateau with a slight sag in the middle.

The last five years under Nelson set five new records in a row ending 1971 with 60,363. This growth was attributed mainly to the low insurance rates of GIA.

During the 12-year Silvers period the records continued to be broken, faltered in 1975, when GIA increased rates on young drivers, and resumed with a new six-year surge from 1976 to the all-time high of 72,806 at the end of 1981. GIA insurance rates were still low, but the main cause of the 12,443 member growth was the Family Farm Water Act. The last four years under Silvers saw a decline of 2,343 due in part to the rising insurance cost of GIA, which was no longer one of the lowest rate companies in the state. By the end of 1983 there were 70,463 Grangers.

For some years Washington stood second to Ohio as the state with the largest state membership. In 1973, Silvers proudly announced that Washington had become the largest state Grange in the nation.

Two aspects of the changing structure of membership data should be noted. The number of Granges peaked at 490 in 1937 and drifted downward to 407 in 1983. But the average Grange size rose from 74 members per Grange in 1937, passed 100 in 1945, reached 125 in 1968, topped at 176 in 1981 and was 173 in 1983. Mainly the Granges were consolidating, but this also reflects total growth of membership since 1937.

Grange community service projects take many forms. One of the largest is Pomona Villa, a retirement housing project sponsored by Pierce County Pomona near Sumner. The project has 40 rental units and other facilities.

The sixth degree rose drill, originated by Agnes Johnson, is a highlight each year for those attending the State Grange convention. This group performed the colorful ceremony at the Grange's diamond anniversary in 1964.

The two main membership lessons of the Silvers period were that membership growth responded to good service, like low GIA rates, and to a call to arms to fight for a good cause, like Initiative No. 59.

Community Service Program. An important responsibility of the Grange is conducting the Community Service Program. For some 15 years the Sears Roebuck Foundation was a sponsor prior to the National Grange taking over.

Both the state and National Granges annually offer savings bonds and certificates to the winning Granges. In 1987, Tekoa Grange in Whitman County won first place in the community service contest. In previous years other Washington Granges have been named national winners.

The philosophy behind these awards was explained by Silvers in both his 1974 and 1976 addresses: "A good community service project will not only benefit your community, but I'm confident it will benefit your Grange as well—for the more we can make our Grange communities realize that ours is an organization that is concerned about others, the better image we will have and more of our neighbors will want to join us."

Grange Leaders and Followers. In 1957, the State Grange delegates launched the annual State Grange Leadership Award. The initial purpose was to pay tribute to outstanding Grange leaders. Noteworthy is the fact that many of the recipients came from small counties at the remote edges of the state. The effect of the award, however, has extended far beyond the 30-some winners to date. More important, the award has called attention to the successful

Anna Slavin

Mary Richmond

Margaret Manda

Mabel Johnston

development of grass-roots leaders throughout the Grange, and in every Grange, and especially among women Grangers. It has also been a way of honoring longtime dedicated members of the Grange staff. Because these particular recipients are representative of the thousands of Grange leaders, the awards honor all Grangers and are a source of pride to all.

In 1977, State Master Jack Silvers presented the leadership award to Agnes Johnson on the 50th anniversary of her achievement in designing the beautiful rose drill of the sixth degree in 1927. The drill is used by state Granges across the nation. Agnes Johnson was State Flora 1923-1933 and again 1943-1947. Her mother, Mrs. Caroline Johnson, brought her six children from Sweden to Redmond in 1906; the father had come a year earlier. They joined Happy Valley Grange No. 322 in 1910. Twice her five singing daughters won the National Grange Talent Contest. Many Granges purchased the two records made by the Johnson sisters containing all the songs of the first four degrees.

In her 1940 history of the Grange, Harriet Ann Crawford worried about the immigrant Germans and Scandinavians being unable to handle the Grange ritual. Mrs. Caroline Johnson would have had a simple answer. She enjoyed attending Grange because it gave her a chance to practice her English. The Grange helped to Americanize the newcomers including the Johnson family.

A legendary Grange leader was Charles F. Keiser (1872-1973), who took part in Grange affairs until past his 100th birthday. He was a leader in forming Chelan County PUD and was a longtime director of GIA. He gave a speech to the National Grange in 1958 on the benefits from public power, and paid tribute to Albert Goss for advocating and achieving both the PUD law and the start of Grand Coulee Dam.

Keiser was 64 when his wife Mattie died in 1936. Ten years later, he married Maybelle King, widow of the late state master. The Leadership Award was given to him in 1959.

At Keiser's 100th birthday party in May 1972, State Master Jack Silvers attended and told Charlie, "I hope I will be able to come back and congratulate you on your 101st birthday too." Charlie leaned to one side as he looked Jack over, then leaned to the other side and replied, "You look pretty healthy to me, Jack. I think you'll make it." Charlie died the next year but his legend lives on.

Dan Jolly served on the state executive committee 33 years from 1948 to 1981. He received the Grange leadership award in 1971. Born on a wheat and cattle farm in 1907 at Leahy, when it took 27 horses to pull the combine, he rented his own farm in 1930, married Harriet Vaughn in 1931, and bought his present 3,207 acres near Connell in 1941, all in wheat. His father Willis celebrated his 100th birthday in 1977.

Dan Jolly became master of St. Andrews No. 832 in 1935 and master of Connell No. 940 in 1940, Pomona master 1949, Franklin County PUD commissioner 1947 to 1970, president of the Northwest Public Power Association, Washington PUD Association, Washington State Power Users Association, Franklin County Hospital District and Franklin County Historical Society. He was a representative in the House 1962 to 1970 and a state senator 1971 to 1976, usually chairing the agricultural committee.

Dan Jolly, Horace Bozarth and Charlie Hodde were among the more recent members representing at least a hundred Grangers who served in the Legislature. Dozens more served as county commissioners, or PUD commissioners. Several went to Congress including Charlie Savage, Walt Horan, Sid Morrison, Knute Hill and Tom Foley. A Hyde Park, New York, Granger even became U.S. President as did a farmer named Harry Truman from Independence, Missouri. The Grange leadership training undoubtedly helped them all to prepare for greater responsibilities. Yet they are but the tip of the much larger iceberg representing the thousands of Grangers who identified and studied problems, developed alternative solutions, proposed resolutions and got the local Grange to deliberate before passing the resolution on to Pomona and then to the State and National Grange committees and delegates. This is the real base of Grange grass-roots legislative effort.

Leadership of Grange Women. Since its founding in 1867, the Grange recognized the membership and voting rights of women. That still left a gender gap for women to overcome, and Washington women Grangers led the way in the effort.

In the August 1987 *Grange News* Avis Beam traces the evolution from the old Women's Work Committee to the Women's Activities Department. By 1936, the name was Home Economics Committee when Maybelle King, wife of the state master, suggested to Anna (Mrs. J.A.) Slavin of Yakima County the need for a more active home economics program. Slavin recommended, and the delegates in 1936 agreed, that home economics be a department of the State Grange with an elected state director. This became the 17th officer of the Washington State Grange. The Home Economics Committee consisted of the state director and seven district directors. In 1969, the name was changed to Women's Activities Department. Anna Slavin headed the department 1937 to 1943, and was followed by Rita Carstens, Pearl Sprinker, Ann Slater, Mary Richmond, Dorothy Stevens and Joy Johnson.

Women's activities are listed in the Grange Handbook and include about 20 programs, projects and contests, many of which end up as extensive displays at State Grange annual sessions.

The women originated the women's breakfast in 1938 and it not only became a regular feature of the annual sessions but also resulted in a men's breakfast the same morning. The annual luncheon of Pomona women leaders originated in 1955.

About half of the officers of the Granges in Washington state are women. Probably in recent years there has been a shift from a slight preponderance of men to a majority of women. Hundreds of women have served as masters of their Granges and many as masters of the Pomona Granges. None as yet has served as state master. Caroline Hall predicted correctly, "Your organization will never be permanent if you leave women out."

Silvers agreed, and he encouraged women to take the lead. Three ladies in particular moved forward in the Silvers era. They have been called "The Three Ms"—Mabel Johnston, Margaret Manda and Mary Richmond.

Mabel Johnston became state lecturer in 1971 serving to 1979. She and her husband Warren had been active Grangers for many years before she took charge of the office of state lecturer. Warren died in April 1981. She again became state lecturer in 1981, serving to 1987. Some of her specialties were the community service award, state and county fair booths and her artistic seed murals.

Henry and Margaret Manda of Yakima came to prominence as state directors of the junior Grange from 1974 to 1981. Margaret had been state chaplain 1967 to 1974, and after 1983 remained active on the Historical Committee.

Mary Richmond served as State Pomona 1961-1971 and director of women's activities 1972-1985. She became a member of the Women's Activities Advisory Committee of the National Grange in 1982. She received the 50-year membership certificate in 1982, and in 1985 the State Grange leadership award. She has remained active in the Grange.

These three fine ladies and a thousand more are but ambassadors representing the vast army of Grange women who, we might as well say it now, really make things happen. Of course they cooked the fine meals, but they also circulated the petitions, contributed and read papers and voiced opinions that counted.

The Economy Turns Down. The first seven or eight years of the Silvers era was a hard act to follow. The 1977 success of the Family Farm Water Act, the all-time record growth in the membership, and becoming the largest State Grange in the nation provided opportunity for happy reminiscences. But not for Jack Silvers. He had to contend with a downturn in agriculture. Farm net income in the U.S. dropped 39 percent in a single year from 1979 to 1980.

Events leading to the 1975-1980 farm disaster started in 1974 when the nation slipped into a generally depressed economy coupled with steep inflation led largely by rising oil prices. It made a shambles of the Jimmy Carter presidency and it got worse when the U.S.S.R. invaded Afghanistan and the U.S. laid an embargo on January 4, 1980, stopping grain shipments to the U.S.S.R. It was hard on Washington grain growers at that time, but the long-term effects were worse as Argentina and other countries added millions of acres of new wheat fields to challenge U.S. exports around the world.

The U.S. Federal Reserve Board then decided on a drastic policy of deflation. The 1982 depression with 11 million unemployed was the result, and it was the most severe economic setback since the Great Depression of 1929 to 1935. The 1982 depression actually began late in 1980 and continued into early 1983. In time the oil conservation efforts of the U.S. began to bear fruit. As the U.S. reduced its oil imports, and as other oil sources entered the world market, the Organization of Petroleum Exporting Countries (OPEC) was unable to maintain its oil price monopoly. A large factor in the economic recovery starting in 1983 was the reduction in the world price of oil.

Somewhat related to the economic gyrations since the Arab-Israel War of 1973 and the resulting oil embargo and price rises was the decline in U.S. public and private investment, which, among many effects, virtually stopped the growth of the electric utility industry.

Electric load rate of growth had reached its postwar peak in 1954 to 1958 but continued at a healthy rate to 1972. After 1972, the growth rate began to slip and falter until, in 1982, the nation used 57 billion kwh less electricity than in 1981. The negative load growth was 2.4 percent. The growing pains of the electric utility industry had become nongrowing pains. The effect was devastating. Between 60 and 100 new generating plants of one million kilowatts each, or larger, that were designed or under construction were first suspended and then canceled outright. Included were eight major TVA plants and nine in the Pacific Northwest. The Washington Public Power Supply System had depended on the electric load forecasts of the Pacific Northwest Utilities Conference Committee. When the forecasts proved to be grossly in error, WPPSS canceled Washington Nuclear Plants (WNP) No. 4 and No.5 and suspended construction on WNP No. 1 and No. 3.

The carrying charges on No. 1 and No. 3 come to about $700 million per year and this has cut into the low cost power tradition of the Pacific Northwest. While electric rates in the region are still only half the national average, the extra cost has been a bitter pill to swallow.

As the time rolled around for the 94th annual session in Everett in 1983, Silvers announced that he did not wish to be reelected. It had been a busy 12 years—a time of victory and much progress and a few setbacks. In his time Washington became the largest State Grange and maintained its reputation as a most progressive State Grange.

CHAPTER THIRTEEN

HILL: 1983 -

STEWARDSHIP OF THE SOIL

"Thou shalt inherit the Holy Earth as a faithful steward, conserving its resources and productivity from generation to generation. Thou shalt safeguard thy fields from soil erosion, thy living waters from drying up, thy forests from desolation, and protect thy hills from overgrazing by thy herds, that thy descendants may have abundance forever. If any shall fail in this stewardship of the land thy fruitful fields shall become sterile stony ground and wasting gullies, and thy descendants shall decrease and live in poverty or perish from off the face of the earth."

The Eleventh Commandment
W.C. Lowdermilk

The terraced hills and mountains of Peru, China, France and dozens of countries testify to the many centuries that farmers around the world have conserved the precious soil. What Lowdermilk did in his remarkable 30-page "Conquest of the Land Through 7,000 Years" was to trace how many countries, once noted for their fertility, have been turned to barren gullies and deserts by bad practices. In 1938 and 1939 he toured a dozen countries to study soil erosion. Earlier for several years he had studied the same problem in China. He became the assistant chief of the Soil Conservation Service of the U.S. Department of Agriculture. His speeches based on his travels appeared in mimeograph form then as a very popular Agriculture Information Bulletin.

Despite the efforts of dedicated farmers and the Soil Conservation Service, the United States is losing millions of acres due to soil erosion. No heavier duty and responsibility falls on the farmers of America and on the members of the Washington State Grange than the protection of the soil. It is a burden that Ray Hill takes very seriously and it is a message that concerns every patriotic American.

Ray Hill was born in The Dalles, Oregon, in 1919. The family moved to Goldendale in 1924 where he grew up on a wheat ranch. He graduated from Washington State University in agricultural economics. He and his wife Helen have three children. He and his son Jim are now partners in operating the Flying H Ranch. Hill was active in many organizations before becoming state master in 1983, and since then has represented the Grange in many more organizations.

He has been a junior Grange master, master of Goldendale Grange No. 49, Pomona master, county deputy since 1961, state overseer 1972-1983, and was elected as the 12th state master in June 1983.

Family Ideal. Central in Hill's thinking is the ideal of the family. With his immediate family as the focus, Hill's thinking radiates outward to become an ever larger and larger family, the individual Grange as a family, the Pomona Grange as a family, the State Grange as a family, the National Grange family, then the community, state, nation and world. The family radiates out to become the universe. The nucleus is the family.

Rural sociologists recognize that the idea of the family evolved with or from the earliest attempts at farming, first from the hunting and fishing life, the nomadic life with domesticated animals and then the settled life of land cultivation. Some trace the origins of civilization to the origins of family life and farming. Thus the human family is the most ancient of all societies and the only one that is natural. It is natural because it is necessitated by the protracted infancy of children. Sociologists say the family is the oldest human institution and the most important.

Ray Hill

Philosophers look on the family as the center of human experience. This is illustrated by the experience of Dr. Robert Maynard Hutchins and his colleagues in compiling *The Great Ideas, a Syntopicon of Great Books of the Western World*. The idea of family was one of their 102 great ideas. Their cross-referencing immediately showed relationships between the family and 21 other great ideas such as love, duty, labor, religion, education, the state, government, nature, war and peace, virtue and vice, monarchy and life and death. Then it became apparent that the family is involved in the total human experience. It is related to each of the other 101 great ideas; it is part of mankind. The Grange is a family organization and stands on a solid footing in calling attention to the family institution, the family way of life and the values inherent in the family ideal. Such values are being eroded in the cities and even in the suburbs. The rural family is a precious resource that should not be overlooked or neglected. It should be cherished.

The Family Farm in Crisis. For a long time it was said that the most important crop of American farms was our sons and daughters. So many farm children had to leave the farm to seek employment elsewhere. The exodus from the land often uprooted the entire family or community. Retirements, foreclosures, droughts and dust storms or simply insufficient income led to farm sales or leasing to a neighbor.

Hill followed the trail so well blazed by Nelson and Silvers in reporting year by year on the trend to bigger farms and fewer farmers. In 1986, Hill reported 2.2 million farms and an estimate that in 14 years there would be another million farms eliminated.

The Grange is fighting back and often has help from Congress and the Internal Revenue Service (IRS). In 1985, Hill reported to the Grangers that an IRS study showed that tax write-offs of farm development costs by nonfarmers exceeded the nation's net farm income.

What this startling fact means is that Congress inadvertently is subsidizing the nonfarmers to help put the legitimate family farm out of business. The Grange contends that a moderately-sized family farm should be able to compete against big corporate farms if the tax laws are fair.

Hill and Silvers pointed out that, unfortunately, the tax laws are often doubly unfair. In addition to tax writeoffs to nonfarmers, Congress makes large subsidies to the corporation super farms. Large farms get the biggest government checks under various so-called farm programs. The reasoning is not that the big farms need the subsidies to survive, but the government needs to obtain the cooperation of the big farms in curbing production.

As farm exports dropped from the all-time record of $43 billion in 1981, the surpluses piled up in the U.S. and farmers were paid to reduce their acreage.

Hill placed much of the blame for the farm problems of the 1980s on the huge military budget, causing large annual deficits. In 1984, he pointed out that the nation took 192 years to incur a national debt of a trillion dollars and then doubled the debt to two trillion dollars in just six years. The result has been high interest rates, which hurt the farmer, and a high priced dollar on foreign exchanges, which hurt U.S. farm exports. Another of Hill's concerns in recent years has been the rise of foreign ownership of U.S. farmland. It is an area the Grange is watching.

The Changing Grange Program. As the Washington State Grange neared its 100th birthday on September 10, 1989, Hill took up several proposals and added some of his own. In 1984, the delegates approved the establishment of a committee to review the State Grange headquarters, which was 50 years old in 1985. The decision was made to move to Olympia. After a study of many building sites, property was purchased near the state Capitol. The move, however, may require several years for selling the Seattle property and building in Olympia. As chairman of the State Grange Centennial Committee, Jack Silvers thinks the State Grange Centennial Day, September 10, 1989, would be a good day for the dedication of the new building.

The State Grange proceeded to sell its interest in Grange Printing, which thereupon became known as Valco Graphics.

The State Grange offices have changed by the addition of computers for word processing, typesetting and accounting.

The efforts to bolster the membership included the adoption of life membership as an innovation. Memorials may be established in honor of a deceased member. Hill takes pride in the increase in endowments to the Grange Foundation. Interest on endowments provides 25 scholarships yearly to deserving students. Four scholarships of $750 are for a four-year period, and the rest are $500 annually.

His interest in soil conservation has been recognized by his being chosen state coordinator by the National Endowment of Soil and Water Conservation in the selection of the State Conservation

The challenge of the '80s and decades beyond is to preserve valuable soil resources for future generations of farmers. USDA Soil Conservation Service photo

Farmer of the Year.

Cherish the Soil. "Every human enterprise is the mixture of a little bit of humanity, a little bit of soil, and a little bit of water." The point of this oft-quoted thought of Jean Brunhes is that the existence of life on the Earth in itself is a miracle, and the existence of human life is a miracle indeed. Moreover, the existence of life depends on a very thin layer of soil. That is why man over the ages has learned to cherish the soil. Unfortunately, the learning process, on how to take care of the soil, has been too slow.

The Threat of Erosion. The Earth produces new soil very slowly—at the rate of about one inch per century. Soil erosion should not be confused with the making of new soil by the erosion of mountains by ice, snow, frost, heat, wind, earthquakes and volcanic action. It took about 40 million years to wear down the first Rocky Mountains; their sediments make up the high plains to the east and west of the present Rocky Mountains. That created a lot of soil.

Washington state has spectacular exhibits to show the work of

Conservation conscious farming results in changed methods and reduced soil loss.

USDA Soil Conservation Service photo

Eastern Washington's Palouse region is particularly susceptible to erosion and annual loss of topsoil due to wind and rain needs to be reduced.

USDA Soil Conservation photo

glaciers and the glacier-fed rivers of the last ice age. The most famous are Grand Coulee, Dry Falls, and the Scablands of eastern Washington. The ancient lava plateau of central Washington over millions of years has gradually become farmland.

The forces of soil erosion are not that slow. The Biblical lands of milk and honey, the Garden of Eden, the Cedars of Lebanon, the legendary Babylon and dozens of other places are no more. Man's mismanagement destroyed the soil.

Gifford Pinchot, chief of the U.S. Forest Service 1898-1910 and later a Grange member and state governor in Pennsylvania, used just two lantern slides to tell the story of what happens when steep mountain slopes are stripped of their forests. One is of a Chinese print of about 600 years ago—a verdant, tree-covered mountain area. The print shows a small saw mill as well. The other slide was a photograph of the same area showing nothing but bare rock.

Not everyone is terrified by the evidence of those advocating soil conservation. The staff of the Hudson Institute in 1976 wrote a book, *The Next Two Hundred Years*, which makes no mention of soil erosion and soil conservation. The food chapter bypasses present ways of obtaining food. It expects us to grow food by hydroponics, without soil, and by creating synthetic foods.

Our Duty to Conserve the Soil. The Middle East countries are not obtaining their food from hydroponics and synthetic sources; they import American agricultural goods or other products from around the world. As much as 40 percent of U.S. farm output has been exported, and it all depends on U.S. soil.

When the Soil Conservation Service celebrated its 50th anniversary in 1985, it was not to announce that the job was done. Despite no-till or minimum-till methods and many other techniques of soil conservation, the SCS is painfully aware that the nation is losing nine to 13 tons of soil per acre each year due to erosion.

Dan Harwood, a St. John area farmer and president of the Pacific Northwest No-Till Association, recently compared soil erosion to a slow nuclear blast. "Our soils are being destroyed at such an astounding rate by erosion," he said, "that there is little difference whether these soils are destroyed by the ultimate weapon or by our own hand." He reported that one-third of the Palouse topsoil is lost. "Conservation tillage and no-till are the only farming techniques which will assure us that we will be successfully farming 800 years down the road."

Each year *The Grange News* publishes a four or eight page section as its annual Conservation Edition. The 37th edition appeared in March 1988. Gone are the days of mere contour plowing and other wasteful methods of soil conservation. Moreover the Congress is increasingly insisting that no agricultural payments may go to farms that do not practice soil conservation. In 1984, Hill told the Grange delegates at Wenatchee:

"Farmers, as stewards of the soil, must be aware that their responsibility goes beyond the farm. Land is one of our most precious resources and must be preserved for future generations if the U.S. is to maintain its status as one of the world's most powerful nations. There will be growing public support for soil conservation and if a farmer benefits from government programs he may be required to conserve soil."

CHAPTER FOURTEEN

PARTNERSHIP WITH NATURE

"In no other country, and at no other time in the history of our own farm economy have so many people been so well provided with such abundance and variety at such low real cost... In short, our farmers deserve praise, not condemnation, and their efficiency should be a cause for gratitude, not something for which they are penalized."

Farm message to Congress
President John F. Kennedy
March 16, 1961

The paradox of farm efficiency is as old as civilization. Civilization became possible when farm efficiency passed the break-even point of mere survival in a world of hunger and famine. When the relentless duties of finding, gathering and preparing food allowed spare time, that spare time could be devoted to the earliest tasks of civilization.

Since the time of the Stone Age the paradox and the challenge have been in how mankind managed that very small amount of spare time from the drudgery chores of hunting and farming. The biggest class of volunteers for the spare time jobs has been the military and they have ever since either forced their rule or managed to persuade their neighbors that the world is full of enemies.

In the first U.S. census of 1790, over 90 percent of the population lived on farms. By the year 1900 the urban population in the U.S. moved ahead of the rural. But in much of the rest of the world the chief occupation was and still is farming.

Kennedy was impressed in 1961 by the enormous productivity of U.S. farmers. Yet in the quarter century since then, the efficiency of farming has again doubled. The farm population has continued to decline. More than two million farms have been merged or discontinued, leaving about 2.2 million farms in the U.S. Hill reported a prediction for loss of another million farms by the year 2000.

An obvious question is whether the remaining farms will be moderate-size family farms or huge corporate or conglomerate corporate farms. This will depend largely on federal tax laws which presently subsidize non-family farm corporations or provide deductions to non-farmers for farm development costs charged to non-farm income. These questions call for public policy decisions.

In Washington state, farming and ranching coexist with spectacular scenery. Supporting a diverse agricultural industry, the state's top 40 crops were worth $3 billion in 1986.
USDA Soil Conservation Service photo

Man and Nature. Such questions fit into the centuries-old study and speculation about the proper balance in the partnership between man and nature, and between farmers and the rest of society. Aristotle (384-322 B.C.) began to systematize the knowledge about man and nature. He had studied under Plato, who had studied man. Aristotle instead decided to study nature. As the teacher for Alexander the Great, Aristotle had the funds to send a thousand explorers and students throughout the Mediterranean world. They began to describe and classify plants and animals. Aristotle developed scientific methods to study natural phenomena.

Agriculture continued to serve as a vast arena for the efforts of mankind to study, understand and better utilize nature. Lucretius saw the broad picture in his book *On The Nature of Things,* when he said, "It follows that with good reason the earth has gotten the name of mother since all things have been produced out of the earth." For 2,000 years natural philosophers studied the physical universe, seeking to understand the relationship of man and nature. They laid the foundation for the agricultural sciences including botany, biology, zoology, and chemistry. In all this time most people were farmers.

Dr. Robert Maynard Hutchins and his colleagues in developing their great books of the Western world found that of the 102 great ideas, there were two that touched all others. They were Man and Nature. This again underlined the depth and universality of the partnership between humans and their world.

Naturalists have had much success in crossbreeding animals and hybridizing plants to improve agriculture. Luther Burbank (1849-1926) was especially skilled in crossing and selection long before the advent of genetics. Among his many developments were the Burbank potato, Shasta daisy and plums.

New Challenges in Education. Research by an Austrian abbot and botanist Gregor Johann Mendel (1822-1884) resulted in Mendel's laws of heredity and led to establishment of genetics as a science. Agricultural colleges and their experimental stations soon applied genetics with notable success in plant improvement. In the state of Washington a series of superior strains of wheat has resulted in sharply increased yields.

The Land Grant College System authorized by the Morrill Act of 1862 has done much more than provide the nation with farm schools, as they were once called. The agricultural colleges of the nation didn't know it at the time, but they had a great advantage. They had to study and deal with the harsh reality of crisis after crisis in American agriculture. When they solved one problem they had to face a dozen more problems. The agricultural colleges dealt with hundreds of agricultural products, extremes of climates and soils, and the many demands of domestic and international trade. The past century brought on waves of revolutionary changes in mechanization, fertilizers, use of chemicals and the continuing structural changes in American agriculture. They were forced to use interdisciplinary approaches that evolved into a total system approach to practical agricultural management. By meeting the continuing challenges of agricultural education many land grant colleges became full-fledged universities. The pragmatic approach was reflected also

Washington's hay production must be large in order to support the state's important cattle industry. Altogether, agriculture-related employers provide jobs for one quarter of the state's workers.

Dave Howard photo

in their extensive input during the last century in farm legislation, and in the series of secretaries of agriculture who came from the land grant colleges.

Washington State University uses interdisciplinary cooperation and coordination across the agricultural studies. The effect has been to broaden the entire curriculum. Most WSU students now come from west of the Cascade Mountains. Entrance requirements are stiff; the evidence is that both WSU and its students try harder.

The Grange has a strong interest in education at all levels, but the relationship with WSU has been special and mutual. Grange conventions at Pullman have also been special starting in 1903, and the seven following conventions have been like homecoming. Thousands of Granger sons and daughters have attended WSU. The centennial of WSU will be in 1990, a year after the State Grange celebration.

Pullman is nestled in the fabulous Palouse country with its endless fields of wheat and other crops. Here, as in farms across the nation, there is a harmony of farm production and the beauties of nature.

Farm Production and Beauty. When one describes the beauties of America, the terms are agricultural. Some think our national anthem should be "America the Beautiful."

"O beautiful for spacious skies.
For amber waves of grain,
For purple mountain's majesty
Above the fruited plain."

The United States has long led the world in agricultural production and has helped many countries to increase their production. American agricultural production has become a hallmark of national pride as well as a symbol of the beauty of America.

Enchanted by his first view of eastern Washington wheat fields, John Gunther in his 1946 book *Inside USA* wrote as if entranced: "I fell asleep in the plane from Seattle to Spokane, and woke up thinking that I must be dreaming. I could not believe what I saw, it was the most beautiful thing I have ever seen in nature. Below us throbbed the wheat. This is undulating country, and the wheat, planted along the hills in eccentric rings and ovals, climbs up one slope and down another. We were flying very low, and the tops of the wheat were intermittently touched by wind; it looked as if somebody were running a gentle invisible thumb over orange plush.

"And the colors! The whole rippling blanket underneath might have been the palette of an artist painting sunsets. The colors are fantastically variegated because the wheat, planted at different times, is ripening at different stages of growth; they run from a deep red-copper through a buttery chrome to gamboge to fawn. Some fields looked like maple leaves and some like richly scrambled eggs. Think of all the red-headed girls you ever met; they are all down there in the wheat—auburn, russet, titian, chestnut, sandy. Then throw in the blondes.

"But these are not the only colors. Look at the browns and greens. The deep sienna brown is just earth. This is because half the acreage must be left fallow each year in this dry part of the world..."

The Future of Agriculture. The futurists visualize some exotic approaches to agriculture. Hydroponics will grow crops without the

Agriculture's future rests in the hands of scientists and researchers such as those working for the College of Agriculture and Home Economics at Washington State University.
WSU photo

need for soil. The laboratory results have been available for decades but no progress has been made to reduce the high costs. Another standard cliche is the growth of plankton in a closed system. Dr. Wayne Rasmussen of USDA mentions these in a recent article but he concludes his look into the next 200 years by quoting the conclusion of his colleague Don Paarlberg in an article of 1975. Paarlberg quoted from the Book of Genesis: "While the earth remaineth, seedtime and harvest, and cold and heat, and summer and winter shall not cease." That is the only prediction as to the future of agriculture. Continued progress in the agricultural sciences and disciplines will achieve better soil conservation, improved plants and animals and good farm management. Predictably, the farmers will continue to become more efficient and will become a yet smaller percentage of the total population.

Grangers will still be the stewards of their farmlands, but the broader partnership of man and nature will increasingly be the concern and responsibility of all citizens.

APPENDIX

Growth and Decline Statistics
Washington State Grange

Year	No. of Granges	Gain or Loss of Granges	No. of Members	Gain or Loss of Members	Average Size of Granges
1888	2	75	—	38	—
1989	15	+13	353	+278	24
1890	27	+12	696	+343	26
1891	35	+8	991	+295	29
1892	36	+1	1,219	+228	34
1893	29	-7	986	-223	34
1894	28	-1	868	-118	31
1895	25	-3	716	-152	29
1896	24	-1	627	-89	27
1897	21	-3	498	-129	24
1898	20	-1	459	-39	23
1899	22	+2	510	+51	23
1900	23	+1	656	+146	29
1901	25	+2	845	+189	34
1902	36	+11	1,298	+453	36
1903	40	+4	1,834	+536	46
1904	52	+12	2,655	+821	51
1905	54	+2	2,813	+158	52
1906	69	+15	3,474	+661	50
1907	90	+21	4,383	+909	49
1908	119	+29	6,347	+1,964	53
1909	184	+65	9,132	2,785	50
1910	260	+76	13,065	+3,933	50
1911	302	+42	15,253	+2,188	51
1912	335	+33	17,029	+1,776	51
1913	317	-18	16,157	-872	51
1914	321	+4	15,445	-712	48
1915	310	-11	13,006	-2,439	42
1916	327	+17	13,206	+200	40
1917	339	+12	14,336	+1,130	42
1918	353	+14	15,622	+1,286	44
1919	319	-34	15,246	-376	48
1920	347	+28	19,367	+4,121	56
1921	363	+16	21,021	+1,654	58
1922	301	-62	14,725	-6,296	49
1923	276	-25	12,321	-2,404	45
1924	272	-4	12,954	+633	48
1925	271	-1	12,879	-75	48
1926	287	+16	14,393	+1,514	50
1927	291	+4	16,762	+2,369	58
1928	307	+16	19,274	+2,512	63
1929	326	+19	20,673	+1,399	63
1930	361	+35	23,100	+2,427	64
1931	389	+28	24,122	+1,022	62
1932	406	+17	23,539	-583	58
1933	420	+14	22,594	-945	54
1934	442	+22	29,134	+6,540	66
1935	466	+24	34,108	+4,974	73

Year	No. of Granges	Gain or Loss of Granges	No. of Members	Gain or Loss of Members	Average Size of Granges
1936	481	+15	36,007	+1,899	75
1937	490	+9	36,428	+421	74
1938	487	-3	36,723	+295	75
1939	488	+1	37,004	+281	76
1940	488	—	36,681	-323	75
1941	485	-3	36,741	+60	76
1942	483	-2	37,202	+461	77
1943	485	+2	38,850	+1,648	80
1944	480	-5	44,793	+5,943	93
1945	476	-4	49,208	+4,415	103
1946	474	-2	51,974	+2,766	110
1947	479	+5	54,813	+2,839	114
1948	482	+3	54,825	+12	114
1949	483	+1	53,240	-1,585	110
1950	483	—	52,217	-1,023	108
1951	481	-2	51,938	-279	108
1952	480	-1	51,258	-690	107
1953	479	-1	50,894	-354	106
1954	480	+1	50,542	-352	105
1955	480	—	50,600	+58	105
1956	479	-1	49,679	-921	103
1957	481	+2	48,667	-1,012	101
1958	481	—	49,137	+470	102
1959	481	-1	50,975	+1,838	106
1960	481	+1	52,553	+1,578	109
1961	478	-3	53,755	+1,022	112
1962	476	-2	54,068	+313	114
1963	475	-1	53,822	-246	113
1964	474	-1	53,865	+43	114
1965	469	-5	53,924	+59	115
1966	468	-1	54,756	+832	117
1967	468	—	56,647	+1,891	121
1968	465	-3	58,264	+1,617	125
1969	463	-2	59,181	+917	128
1970	460	-3	60,070	+889	131
1971	457	-3	60,363	+293	132
1972	452	-5	61,386	+1,023	136
1973	443	-9	62,018	+632	140
1974	443	—	62,627	+609	141
1975	438	-5	61,752	-875	141
1976	432	-6	62,321	+569	144
1977	425	-7	66,034	+3,713	155
1978	422	-3	69,042	+3,008	164
1979	419	-3	71,258	+2,216	170
1980	418	-1	72,663	+1,405	174
1981	413	-5	72,806	+143	176
1982	411	-2	71,400	-1,406	174
1983	407	-4	70,463	-937	173
1984	405	-2	68,782	-1,681	170
1985	403	-2	66,659	-2,123	165
1986	403	—	63,774	-2,885	158
1987	401	-2	60,078	-3,696	150

Washington State Grange Officers 1987-1988

MASTER: Ray Hill
OVERSEER: Robert Clark
LECTURER: Wilma Baker
STEWARD: Dennis Hall
ASSISTANT STEWARD: Tom McKern
LADY ASSISTANT STEWARD: Helen Gardner
CHAPLAIN: Sylvia Crumpler
TREASURER: June Hendrickson
SECRETARY: Codi Titus
GATEKEEPER: Duane Hamp
CERES: Cheryl Chapin
POMONA: Cheryl Cowell
FLORA: Helen Erkenbrack
EXECUTIVE COMMITTEE:
Bill Crow
Jack Silvers
Steve Krupke
WOMEN'S ACTIVITIES DIRECTOR: Joy Johnson
YOUTH DIRECTOR: Tom Gwin
JUNIOR DIRECTORS: Wayne and Peggy Miller

Grange Leadership Award Winners

1957—W.T. Smith, manager of Grange Cooperative Wholesale
1958—Fred Nelson, state master, Grange Cooperative Wholesale
1959—Charles F. Keiser, Grange Insurance Association
1960—Horace W. Bozarth, state legislator, Grange Cooperative Wholesale
1961—John Dobie, Grange Cooperative Wholesale, conservationist
1962—Charles Hodde, State Grange deputy and overseer, state legislator, Dept. of Revenue director
1963—Max Schmuck, public utility district leader, conservationist
1964—Ira E. Shea, State Grange lecturer, deputy, Grange Mutual Life
1965—J.R. Ayers, Grange leader, Research Committee member
1966—Adda Ruth Roberts, State Grange secretary, chaplain, deputy
1967—Frank O. Miller, State Grange overseer, executive committee, legislator, Grange Supply manager
1968—J.T. Danaher, cooperative builder, agriculturist
1969—Ted A. Lloyd, State Grange deputy, agriculturist
1970—Lena Lloyd, State Grange junior director
1971—Dan Jolly, State Grange executive committee, state senator
1972—Ted F. Berry, editor of *The Grange News*
1973—Thora Dick, State Grange junior director
1974—Martin Auseth, county commissioner, deputy
1975—Avis Beam, assistant editor of *The Grange News*
1976—Irma Smith, secretary to the state master
1977—Agnes Johnson, rose drill originator, state Flora

1978—Chester Crandall, State Grange executive committee, Pomona master
1979—Bob Elwess, State Grange youth director
1980—Frieda Berger, State Grange lecturer
1981—Gerald Fenton, deputy, public utility district commissioner
1982—Eleanor Dudonsky, state Ceres
1983—Ray Schneider, State Grange executive committee, deputy
1984—Homer Trefry, county and legislative deputy, county commissioner
1985—Mary Richmond, state director of women's activities, deputy
1986—Jim Miller, State Grange deputy, Pomona master
1987—Vance Arter, State Grange deputy
1988—Mabel Johnston, State Grange lecturer, Grange Day fair coordinator

Washington State Agriculture
Top 40 Commodities
Value of Production

1.	Apples	$489,280,000
2.	Milk	468,980,000
3.	Wheat	297,968,000
4.	Cattle and calves	294,337,000
5.	Potatoes	252,756,000
6.	Hay	173,877,000
7.	Nursery/greenhouse products	90,000,000
8.	Barley	74,250,000
9.	All pears	72,754,000
10.	Sweet cherries	59,437,000
11.	Hops	57,504,000
12.	Eggs	55,577,000
13.	Asparagus	40,612,000
14.	Grapes	37,120,000
15.	Chickens and broilers	36,049,000
16.	Corn, grain	35,700,000
17.	Corn, silage	27,000,000
18.	Lentils	26,637,000
19.	Mint oil	25,509,000
20.	Sweet corn, all	24,531,000
21.	Onions	23,770,000
22.	Green peas, processing	20,431,000
23.	Dry edible Peas	18,054,000
24.	Kentucky bluegrass seed	13,407,000
25.	Carrots	12,270,000
26.	Dry edible beans	12,127,000
27.	Alfalfa seed	10,537,000
28.	Red raspberries	10,509,000
29.	Peaches	8,760,000
30.	Mink	8,085,000
31.	Hogs	7,227,000
32.	Strawberries	6,500,000
33.	Mushrooms	6,263,000
34.	Cranberries	5,550,000
35.	Sheeps, lambs, & wool	3,696,000
36.	Prunes	3,329,000
37.	Apricots	3,319,000
38.	Lettuce	3,175,000
39.	Wrinkled seed peas	2,498,000
40.	Oats	2,467,000

TOTAL VALUE OF PRODUCTION *$3 BILLION*

Washington Agricultural Statistics Service, 1986

BIBLIOGRAPHY

The availability of good bibliographies on American agricultural history is owing to the joint effort of the USDA Agricultural History Branch, headed by Dr. Wayne D. Rasmussen, and the University of California at Davis Agricultural History Center directed by Dr. Alan L. Olmstead. Among 26 bibliographies issued 1963-1980, the following were used. They are listed as publications of the Agricultural History Center at Davis, which also publishes the quarterly magazine *Agricultural History*.

Agricultural History Center, University of California at Davis, "Agricultural History, An Index 1927-1976," Sept. 1977, 100 p. The magazine is available either on microfilm or as shelf copy at Washington State University at Pullman.

-----"A Preliminary List of References for the History of the Grange Movement," Nov. 1967, 21 p. This was prepared incident to the National Grange Centennial. The compiler, Dennis S. Nordin, points out that Solon Buck's 1913 *The Granger Movement* had been the "classic" source on the Granger movement, with an extensive bibliography. But it covers the general farm unrest of 1870 to 1880 and is not really a history of the Grange. A second comment by Nordin is that little has been written about Grange history since 1880.

-----"A Selected Bibliography on George Washington's Interest in Agriculture," Jan. 1976, 46 p. He has been called the father of scientific agriculture.

-----"A List of References for the History of the Farmers' Alliance and the Populist Party," June 1973, 80 p. Washington's Populist Governor John R. Rogers is mentioned.

Buck, Solon Justus. *The Granger Movement, A study of agricultural organization and its political, economic, and social manifestations, 1870-1880,* Cambridge: Harvard University Press, 1913. Reprinted by University of Nebraska Press, 1963. Buck's pessimism about the Grange appears justified based on the history to 1913. He could not foresee the favorable U.S. Supreme Court decisions issued in and after 1934 and the revival of the National Grange from a dormant period.

Crawford, Harriet Ann. *The Washington State Grange, A Romance of Democracy, 1889-1924,* Portland, Ore.: Binfords & Mort, 1940, bibliography 324-332.

1. Embattled Farmers Form Granges

Carstensen, Vernon, Ed. *Farmer Discontent 1865-1890,* New York: Wiley, 1974 Biblio note 181-184.

Edwards, Everett E. *Washington, Jefferson, Lincoln and Agriculture,* Washington D. C.: 1937.

Kelley, Oliver H. *Origin and Progress of the Patrons of Husbandry in the United States, A history from 1866 to 1873,* Philadelphia: 1875.

Rasmussen, Wayne D. *Agriculture in the United States, A Documentary History,* 4 v. New York: Random House, 1975.

------Editor. *Readings in the History of American Agriculture,* Urbana: University of Illinois Press, 1960. Chronology, selected readings.

Martin, Edward Winslow. *History of the Grange Movement; or the Farmer's War Against Monopolies,* Chicago: 1874.

Winders, Gertrude Hecker. *Horace Greeley: Newspaperman,* New York: John Day Co., 1962.

2. The Grange's Greatest Victory

The National Grange, Legal and Economic Influence of The Grange 1867-1967, prize-winning essays by law students on the impact of the Grange on social legislation, with introductory statement by Judge Thurman Arnold. Washington, D.C.: The National Grange, 1967, 98 p.

The National Grange. *Journal of the Proceedings,* 100th Annual Session, Minneapolis, Minnesota, November 17, 1966, Washington, D.C.: The National Grange, 1967.

3. The First Farm in Washington State

Gibson, James R. *Farming the Frontier: the Agricultural Opening of the Oregon Country 1786-1846,* Vancouver: University of British Columbia Press, 1985. Notes and bibliography. The definitive source, competent and comprehensive.

Merk, Frederick. *Fur Trade and Empire, George Simpson's Journal 1824-25,* Cambridge: Harvard University Press, 1931, revised 1968.

Pacific Northwest Quarterly and *Oregon Historical Quarterly* have many articles on farming activities of the Hudson's Bay Company and its subsidiary Puget Sound Agricultural Co.

4. Oregonians Fight Monopoly

Buisman, Ben. "75 Years of Service to Oregon Farmers 1875-1948," *Oregon Grange Bulletin* supplement, Vol. 53, No. 9., Oct. 5, 1948, 32 p.

Oregon State Grange, *Organization and Proceedings of the First Session of the Oregon State Grange,* Salem, Oregon: Sept. 24-27, 1873, p. 23, printed 1906. Reproduced March 1973 by Washington State Grange Historical Committee in Oregon State Grange Proceedings 1873-1892. As many as 72 Granges in Washington Territory were part of the Oregon State Grange during the 1873-1889 period prior to the creation of the Washington State Grange.

------"The Oregon State Grange—A History of Accomplishment," *Oregon Grange Bulletin,* Nov. 5, 1985, p. 17-18.

Scott, Edna A. "The Grange Movement in Oregon 1873-1900" M.A. Thesis, University of Oregon, 1923.

5. Farmers Organize on the Washington Frontier

Avery, Mary W. *History and Government of the State of Washington,* Seattle: University of Washington Press, 1961.

Fite, Gilbert C. "Daydreams and Nightmares; The Late Nineteenth Century Agricultural Frontiers" 1966 *Agr. Hist.* No. 4, p. 285.

Gates, Charles Marvin, Ed. *Messages of the Governors of the Territory of Washington to the Legislative Assembly 1854-1889,* Seattle: University of Washington Press, 1940.

Washington State Grange, *Proceedings of the Annual Session,* Seattle: Washington State Grange, 1889-present. The annual *Proceedings* evolved from 26 pages in 1889 to an average of 300 in recent years. Each is centered on the Master's Address, which likewise has evolved from five printed pages to over 40. The sessions have grown from three to five working days. The *Proceedings* includes the financial report for the year, membership changes, the executive committee minutes and generally a documentation of policy making decisions.

6. By Their Deeds and by Their Words

Ellsworth, Clayton S. "Theodore Roosevelt's Country Life Commission," 1960, *Agr. Hist.* 34: 155-172.

Johnson, Claudius O. "The Adoption of the Initiative and Referendum in Washington," *Pacific Northwest Quarterly,* Vol. 35, Oct. 1944, p. 291-303.

------"The Initiative and Referendum in Washington," *Pacific Northwest Quarterly,* Vol. 36, Jan. 1945, p. 29-63.

King, Judson. *The Conservation Fight, From T. R. to the T.V.A.,* Washington D.C.: Public Affairs Press, 1959.

LaPalombara, Joseph G. *The Initiative and Referendum in Oregon 1930-1948,* Corvallis, Ore.: Oregon State College Press, 1950.

Munro, W.B. *The Initiative, Referendum and Recall,* New York: D. Appleton & Co., 1912.

Thompson, C.J. "The Origin of Direct Legislation in Oregon," M.A. Thesis, Eugene: University of Oregon, 1929.

U.S. Country Life Commission, *Report of the Country Life Commission,* 1909, 65 p. U.S. 60th Cong., 2nd sess., Senate Doc. 705.

7. To Make Us Bear With Patience.

Manuscript Library, University of Washington. Papers of William Morley Bouck 1868-1945, about two inches, letters, diary, clips, ephemera.

Schwantes, Carlos A. "Farmer-Labor Insurgency in Washington State," *Pacific Northwest Quarterly,* Jan. 1985, Vol. 76. No. 1. p. 2-11. Good footnotes.

------"Making the World Unsafe for Democracy," *Montana,* The Magazine of Western History, Sept. 1981, Vol. 31. Winter, p. 19-29.

------*Radical Heritage: Labor, Socialism and Reform in Washington and British Columbia, 1885-1917,* Seattle: University of Washington Press, 1979.

------"The Ordeal of William Morley Bouck, 1918-1919; Limits to the Federal Suppression of Agrarian Dissidents" July 1985 *Agr. Hist.* Vol. 59, No. 3. P. 417-428.

8. Grangers Write A Law

Bertels, Sister M. Thomas More. "The National Grange—Progressives on the Land, 1900 - 1930" Ph. D. Thesis, Washington D.C.: Catholic University of America, 1962. Biblio, notes.

Bertels seldom finds the National Grange progressive in the 1900-1930 period. In her later writings and speeches at The National Grange she was pleased to report that The National Grange had restored its early image for progressiveness.

Goss, Albert. *Current Biography*, March 1945, p. 241-243, Obituary in Dec. 1950 issue.

------Letter of March 14, 1940, Albert S. Goss to *Grange News* Editor Ted F. Berry explaining Goss' resignation as Land Bank Commissioner.

The National Grange. "A Tribute to the Memory of Albert S. Goss, Master of The National Grange 1941-1950," The National Grange 1951, 25 p.

9. Developing Cooperative Enterprise

The Grange News, June 1935. Features dedication of Grange headquarters building.

------June 10, 1939, four sections. Celebrates the Grange golden anniversary with articles featuring Grange history and activities.

Norwood, Gus. *Columbia River Power For The People*, a history of policies of the Bonneville Power Administration, Portland, Ore.: Bonneville Power Administration, 1981. Chronology and bibliography. Includes historical background on the federal power program.

Schlesinger, Arthur M. Jr. *The Age of Roosevelt*, 3 v. Boston: Houghton Mifflin Co. 1957-1960.

Shea, Ira E., *The Grange Was My Life*, Fairfield, Wash.: Ye Galleon Press, 1983.

10. Building the Grange in War and Peace

The Grange News, September 1945, and Nov. 17, 1945. These issues featured the role of Washington Grangers in World War II.

------, Dec. 19, 1952. Special section on "The PUD Story."

Gray, Henry L. "Some Aspects of Public Utility Condemnation Cases," paper presented to American Society of Civil Engineers, Seattle, July 22, 1948. Includes table on 19 cases.

Author's file on condemnation includes several BPA internal memoranda 1946 to 1950 on condemnation awards both accepted and rejected.

11. In the Public Interest

Lyons, Barrow *Tomorrow's Birthright*, a political and economic interpretation of our natural resources, New York: Funk & Wagnalls Co., 1955.

12. Winning the Family Farm Water Struggle

Agricultural Grange News, Oct. 1, 1912, Feature article on "Pioneer Roads."

Powell, John Wesley. *Report on the Lands of the Arid Region of the United States*, Washington: GPO, 1879.

Stegner, Wallace. *Beyond the Hundredth Meridian—John Wesley Powell and the Second Opening of the West*, Boston: Houghton Mifflin, 1954.

13. On Being A Faithful Steward

Brink, Wellington. *Big Hugh, The Father of Soil Conservation*, New York: 1951.

Hutchins, Robert Maynard, Editor, *Great Books of the Western World*, 54 vol. Chicago: Encyclopaedia Britannica, 1952.

Lowdermilk, W.C. "Conquest of the Land Through Seven Thousand Years," Agr. Info. Bull. No. 99, USDA Soil Conservation Service, 1942, printed 1953.

14. Partnership With Nature

Paarlberg, Don. "Agriculture Two Hundred Years From Now" *Agr. Hist.* 50 (January 1976), 309.

Rasmussen, Wayne D. "Agriculture in the Future," *Red River Valley Historical Review*, vol. 3, no. 1 (Winter 1978), p. 9-22.

INDEX

About the author—

Author Gus Norwood first approached the project of compiling a history of the centenary of the Grange in Washington as an expert. Perhaps the most significant accomplishment of the Washington State Grange during its first 100 years was implementation of publicly-owned utilities—Washington's public utility districts. Norwood had personal experience with this development as the first executive secretary for the Northwest Public Power Association. After 20 years in this post, he was appointed the first administrator of the Alaska Power Administration and he subsequently served briefly with the Atomic Energy Commission in Maryland. In 1974 Norwood returned to the Pacific Northwest as an employee of the Bonneville Power Administration in Portland. While there he wrote a history of BPA policies, *Columbia River Power for the People,* released in 1981. He retired later that year. Born in Chicago in 1916, Norwood was educated at Elmhurst College, the U.S. Naval Academy and Harvard University where he received his master's in public administration. Elmhurst granted him an honorary Doctor of Law degree in 1983. Norwood and his wife Jean live in Vancouver, Washington, where he is a 40-year member of the Grange and current president of the Fort Vancouver Historical Society.